The author was born in Scotland in 1946 to a large family of 11 children. At the age of 16 Alice moved to London to work for the Royal Household, whilst there she met her future husband, a member of the Household Cavalry. Alice has three grandchildren.

This book is a tribute to my husband, Tony Taft, who died just after the manuscript of this work was completed. Also in memory of my sister, Mary, and my brother, Geordie.

Alice Taft

A DIFFERENT LIFE

AUSTIN MACAULEY
PUBLISHERS LTD.

A CIP catalogue record for this title is available from the British Library.

ISBN 978 1 84963 905 7

www.austinmacauley.com

First Published (2015)
Austin Macauley Publishers Ltd.
25 Canada Square
Canary Wharf
London
E14 5LB

Printed and bound in Great Britain

Chapter 1

A Different Life

Little did I realise while walking through the small wood with the dry crackling branches beneath my feet and the glorious sight of the trees, snowdrops and daffodils that it would create a memory which would last a lifetime. This was at the age of seven when my world had already been so tumbled and mysterious for reasons that to me were hard to understand.

My earliest memories are of a life that was, and from then on would be, changed forever. Our home was on the outskirts of a small village called Auchnagatt in the County of Aberdeen. My father was a farm worker with poor wages, so we had little money and very substandard housing. It pains me to say or think it, but my parents lacked the stamina and energy needed to cope with the task of raising a large family. We were six girls and five boys; myself, Alice, eighth child of Colin and Helen Young; my sisters Mary, Bunty, Meg, Betty, Chrissie; and my brothers Sandy, Colin, Geordie, Willie and John. An added complication was my father's eyesight; he was suffering a rapid deterioration in his vision, leading to our mother having to work with him some of the time on the farm to keep his house and his job because we lived in farm houses for farm workers. The family home was an "L" shaped cottage. We had the main side and the father of the farmer, a kindly man we affectionately called 'Old Tom', had the smaller end. The cottage was set in a close with no other houses in sight. We had two bedrooms, a living room and a kitchen, which was really much too small for a family of thirteen. The toilet was housed outside and as with many houses at that time there was no electricity or hot water. On the wall outside our old tin bath would hang and the mangle was just outside the door. I do have some memories of those

7

early years, such as how we would walk to a copper bridge and spend many hours playing by the burn, the older children looking after us younger ones. This would have been Meg, Geordie and Betty as Colin, Sandy, Mary and Bunty would have been working, the boys in farm work and the girls in farm houses, that was until Colin was called up for National Service and went to join The Gordon Highlanders.

In the evenings the tilley lamps would be lit, I liked to see them made ready to hang on the hooks on the ceiling to give us light. I would watch the new mantle being fitted, I thought it pretty in pink and white mesh, so clear a memory. I can picture us at the table, the younger ones at the back by the wall, as there was not enough chairs for everyone, listening to our Mum and Dad discuss our heights and how we had grown. This was one of the many little snatches of conversation that would become important to me, assuring me that they loved us and didn't mean for it to go so wrong.

Our Mum loved reading and spent too long doing just that; she often would sit and teach us simple verse from a book. I felt language was important to her and can remember being corrected more than once on something I said, such as when I said 'me and Betty', "it should be Betty and I" she would say, I felt she liked us to talk nicely.

Our village school had only two classrooms, one for Mrs Menzies, our head teacher, and the other for Miss Keith, her assistant. I can picture a scene in our classroom one day when I felt it unfair to be told off. I was accused of being destructive when caught examining a pencil I had found on the floor. This yellow and black stripe pencil had been cut lengthwise in half, I was examining the lead, I hadn't split it but I was blamed. This stayed in my memory.

As I was the youngest girl in school I was chosen to present flowers to a guest at a special event the school was holding in the Church Hall. For this day Mrs Menzies gave me a dusky blue velvet dress to wear, I loved it as it felt so nice and made me feel very pretty. After the presentation I was invited to be the first child to pick a present from a Santa who had a special coat with lots of pockets, each one holding a present, I can hear now the lady guest say 'she's so sweet'. She gave me a kiss and said

I was to choose a second gift, wow lucky me! Betty tells me Mrs Menzies favoured me and during holiday times would have me stay at her house for a few days, yet I have no recollection of this.

Other "stay in my mind" events were seeing my Dad and older brothers all dressed in black clothing, I believe this was to attend the funeral of one of my grandmothers, or another time gathered in the close ready to go to the famous horse market Aikey Brae. Pictures of these scenes stay in my mind, I now know men and young lads looking for work would attend these events where farmers would hire labourers as needed.

We were a very close and loving family with a unique bond of love that was forever a very great part and strength which became etched on every family member. This was a very important factor in our lives creating a strong spirit in every one of us in these carefree years. Little did we know how much we would have to draw on these strengths to help us through the years ahead when times were often hard and cruel. We had no knowledge that our family lives were being monitored and big changes were about to be put in place.

These changes happened in 1953, I was six years old at this time. Everyone was up early as it was normally a school day. It felt as if there was an air of excitement with a strange atmosphere, we had all been bathed the night before and more attention than usual paid to the clothes we were wearing to make us appear tidy in our 'hand me down clothes'. Our Mum, Dad, Willie, Chrissie and John went off in a car while Geordie, Meg, Betty and I set off on a three mile walk to the station. It was early this cold and wintry February morning and there was plenty of snow on the ground.

We met some of our friends on their way to school who of course wanted to know where we were going, Geordie gave them the reply 'we're going to South America', same question from another group 'Timbuktu' says Geordie.

I'm not sure what the older ones thought or knew of the day ahead, as for me, I had no idea, I expect I thought it was some big exciting adventure, it seemed that way. Little did I know what lay ahead for me and my family, that day itself was very strange and unreal, with only some of the day clear in my mind.

We were actually on our way to a court hearing in the seaside town of Peterhead. As we got off the train we could feel the winds icy blast blowing off the North Sea as we made our way through the streets towards the Magistrates Court and were very glad to get inside and feel the warmth of the building, where we were led to a room to sit and wait. I don't have much memory of being in the courtroom, for Betty being four years older it was a bit clearer, she could picture the setup of the room. The Magistrate, social worker, Probation Officer, three or four other officials and our parents were in serious discussion with arguments, sometimes heated, about the home conditions for the children. Betty, like Meg and Geordie, wondered what all the fuss was about. We lived in a happy home where we were loved, while us four younger ones had no idea what it was all about.

The future for the children was decided and plans put in place.

For me our Mum and Dad were just no longer there, I hadn't seen them go, though Betty did see our Mum look back and wave as we were led away. So there were no words of reassurance or comfort for us. I had no idea this would mean we would never live with our Mum and Dad again, that we would leave behind Mary, Bunty, Sandy and Colin, and would have to face a very uncertain future.

We were taken on what seemed a long journey into Aberdeen to the welfare office where we had even more waiting around and were eventually given a lunch of tomato soup and bread. They were later to discover that this had not been a very good idea because as we were unused to cars we were all very travel sick and any future journey would include towels and bowls.

I had no idea where Geordie, Meg, Willie and John went, but Chrissie and I were taken on another journey to Banchory to a home called Linn Moor. Betty said she too was there, perhaps in a wing for older ones as I can only think of Chrissie and I being bathed and having our hair washed and made ready for bed.

It had been a very long and exhausting day for us we felt so alone and lost, Chrissie was only four and felt frightened and came into my bed during the night. She was told off for this, I felt this was really mean.

It seems we were there only a very short time, I do have a memory of us being given some pretty ribbons for our hair, mine green, Chrissie's red. Each morning we would have to line up and were given a spoonful of castor oil, of course we hated this, as did all the other children.

Soon after we were being made ready to move again, this time back into Aberdeen to another children's home called The Children's Shelter. We were delighted to see Willie and John were there, John was only three and Willie five.

Again our stay was short, I do have some memories of this place, and I can picture the dining room with little tables and chairs for four, some tables with yellow tops and some with blue. Again each day we would have the castor oil line up and noted some older kids would change queue to dodge having it, I don't expect this always worked. I can also see us lined up in twos ready to go out each day, I'm not sure where to, a school perhaps.

My worst time was the nights when the dormitories felt so dark and scary. I used to cry myself to sleep after searching the room to find a chink of light I could focus on to comfort me because if I was heard crying I would be told not to be silly and to go to sleep.

Once again as usual with no explanation it was time for our next move. I really can't give details of how long or short each stay was, I didn't register times and dates it was all so confusing. This time the journey was longer for us, actually only two hours, but with the need for towels and bowls in place it felt much longer. We were out in the country again the children's home called Cobblehaugh in a nice setting at the foot of Bennachie. This was yet another short stay while our future home was being made ready for us.

Chapter 2

The Old Manse

The day came for that move, thankfully a very short car journey. We were in the small village of Culsamond in Aberdeenshire.

We arrived to be driven through some tall iron gates and on to see a very impressive old house. Our real delight was to see Meg, Geordie and Betty, which meant that together with Willie, Chrissie, John and I, all of us who had left home were together again. This was very special, we were a close family who needed to be together.

The house was called The Old Manse. First we were introduced to the owners, Mr and Mrs McMaster, and their young daughter Rosemary then their friend Mrs Humphries who we were told would cook all our meals. We were shown round all the rooms we would use. There was a long corridor which at one end had two playrooms. We would use the smaller one. Leading off the corridor was a bathroom and toilet and a lovely big wide staircase. At the other end there was a pantry and an older staircase to the older part of the house which we wouldn't as yet use. There was a big kitchen with a big table where we would eat our meals. Our dormitories were up the big grand staircase.

Once settled we were asked if we would like to walk around the grounds, this was to be only two at a time. It was here we walked through this delightful wood, it was so lovely and created a memory I would store in my heart and mind forever, the trees, snowdrops and daffodils gave me much pleasure.

There were of course some house rules, Meg, Betty and Geordie were told of their tasks expected of them, every morning Meg was to make the porridge for breakfast and Betty would set the table and wash up, she also reminded me of the task she hated most, this was to wash all the hankies. Geordie was to clean all the shoes. Meg and Betty were also responsible for the bathing of the younger ones.

This was the start of what was to be a three year stay and, I feel, a very special part of our childhood. Culsamond Primary was a twenty minute walk from the Manse. Meg, Geordie and, later, Betty would bike the three miles to Insch School.

The Manse was a lovely old house set in its own beautiful grounds. There was a small wood and at the front of the house there was an area with a big flagstone terrace and on one side a grassed area that led to the wood.

The house was long and impressive, the property enclosed with railings and black iron gates.

The food cooked by Mrs Humphries was most likely very good, however being presented with some foods we were unused to was often a challenge, I can especially remember the stew and dumplings – we hated those! One day we were served this, the rule being no one could leave the table till plates were empty, this was just not going to happen so Geordie had a plan! He opened the window, made a hole in the earth and buried them and joked about a dumpling tree that would grow there in years to come – so you have been warned!

We had many adventures at the Manse, us younger ones loving simple play such as crushing corn to make flour or picking clover and rose petals to make perfume, these were mostly happy days in our lives. Bedtimes became special to us because when the lights went out Meg would make up the most wonderful stories, we really loved them, they would continue each night keeping us enthralled and eager for the next night. Meg was very gifted at this, making bedtimes feel like our very own special and secret times. We would always consider this to be our special time, and so much inspired by these stories Chrissie and I would continue them at school playtimes or in the Manse grounds.

On Sundays we would attend church and Sunday school and would have permission to have a walk outside the grounds later in the day. On these walks we would often pick roadside country treats such as birds foot trefoil known to us as 'birdies peas' or sorrel known as 'souricks'. Other times we'd choose a fresh turnip from the field, crack and break it on stones and share it to enjoy the fresh succulent taste, these to us were delicious treats, sometimes we'd meet and chat with friends, just being together was important to us having endured the pain and anxieties of separation already, we were a close and emotional family and really knew how to pull together.

Mr and Mrs McMaster had many influential friends who would visit, one couple I especially remember were Mr and Mrs Haughton of Williamston House. Mrs Haughton was a very grand lady who was to make a very big impression on me. She would call into our bedroom to say 'hello' and at one time gave me a memorable lesson on how a young lady should leave her discarded clothes and made me tidy them in a certain order, I took this to heart and it became a rule I continue to this day.

One year during summer holidays we were invited by Mr and Mrs Haughton to have a picnic in the grounds of Williamston House. The estate was outstandingly beautiful, the scene so lovely with swans looking so graceful on a lake and peacocks strutting around the grounds. One of the peacocks came near to me while I was eating a sandwich and as I was a little scared of it I chased it away. This was seen by Mrs Haughton who told me off with a little rhyme saying:

"If you be rude to my beasts
Then I'll be rude to you
If you be good to my beasts
Then I'll be good to you."

These words I have always remembered though we did repeat and laugh over it later. She was also very quick to pick us up over our stance making us pull our shoulders back and stand up straight. Indeed a very formidable lady for whom I held much respect.

Staying with us at the Manse for some of the time was a teenage lad from Port Glasgow, Billy Dunsmore. Billy used to get into a lot of trouble and went to a special school. Also, for a fairly short stay a twin boy and girl joined us, they were Mary and Dennis. There was always a lot going on.

Life went on at the Manse, mostly it felt like a good time in our lives, though at some times we did suffer some hurt and humiliation, like the time we somehow got the idea we were going home to our Mum and Dad. On hearing this was untrue Geordie became quite enraged and I could see him kicking a metal tea pot along the corridor in anger and frustration, this of course was a punishable offense and we were all smacked on the legs with a cane leaving angry welts.

Mary and Bunty came to visit us at one time and noted we had marks on our legs. It was nice that they could come and keep in touch with us.

Many times I was chosen to go to the McMasters' private quarters to play with Rosemary. It was while there one day when our next punishment was to happen. Mrs McMaster came through with a book to show me. She was cross because she had found a neatly cut out Santa. She asked if I had done it, I said 'no I hadn't', but felt it could not have been done by a younger child as it was too neat. She said 'sorry Alice as no one will own up to this destruction all must be punished' and she gave me two lashes of the cane on my hand, this time right there in front of Rosemary, I felt this very unfair as I always resented punishment for things I hadn't done.

Chapter 3

Winter Days

The winter weather in Scotland could often be very severe. Young people today would laugh at the amount of clothes we would wear: our vest, then liberty bodice, before our top and pinafore. I'm not sure where we lived when I remember these pink camphor pads which we would put next to our chest, I think it may only have been when we had colds, I just remember them.

I have to say I felt a special love for the elaborate leaf patterns created by the frosts, the shapes fascinated me, I rather miss these to this day and the big icicles, all eliminated by central heating.

One day the snow was very deep, making it impossible for most to attend school. We did manage to plod through it to get there, but only one other family made it, it felt very strange and fun in the empty classroom with reading as our only lesson, I loved to read. I was most impressed to see the small bottles of milk provided for break, the iced milk stood high above the bottles with the little red foil tops all still on, it looked strange and fascinating to me.

The snow continued to fall and the school closed early even then it was clear we could not walk home, the snow was so deep we would have been buried. We were told to wait to be picked up, this was a tractor and cart to take us through the field to the Manse, great fun for us!

In springtime our friends, the Hendersons, invited us to their small farm where we were able to feed these gorgeous piglets and hold some new fluffy chicks, we loved that and their Mum gave us homemade lemonade and cakes.

One day I woke up with a very sore throat, this was not the first time, so the Doctor was sent for. He decided I needed to have my tonsils taken out. Rather strangely, all six of us went into Huntley hospital for the same procedure! We had a ward to ourselves, when I woke after the operation I was very upset to see my sisters and brothers all eating ice cream, sleeping longer I had missed out.

In our ward I was opposite the open door and could see along the corridor. In the end ward was a man with one leg, each day he waved and smiled to me, I considered him a friend, yet at night I would cry as I was scared of the man with one leg – silly girl! Of course the night nurse told me off for this.

Strange, the memories that stay in your mind, like when we got new dresses. Chrissie and I had white waffle-look dresses with a sort of crisp feel; we called them our paper dresses. Each dress had a band of colour at the bottom with flowers around the band, mine green, Chrissie's red. They felt very special, we loved them. Meg and Betty had flared circular dresses, when out for our walk they would twirl round to make them flare out, I thought them very glamorous and rather envied such a dress.

When it was our birthday we were given a shilling and would get Meg and Geordie to stop at the shop on their way to school and buy whatever sweets you got most of for the shilling. It would sometimes be farthing chews or a big coloured circular candy wheel as we liked those and could share with each other, mostly nicely I think!

Meg wrote plays with parts for us all to act. Mr and Mrs McMaster invited their friends to come to see them, this would include Mr and Mrs Haughton, the minister, and local headmaster. The Bishop of Inverurie would come too so they became very important events that kept us all amused. Meg was very good and enthusiastic at putting these together. Christmas time it would be the nativity and Miss Humphries would make mince pies, not that I liked them! When she made the Christmas cake she would let us stir the mixture and make a wish.

A box of toys would be delivered, I've no idea where from, we would all have something for Christmas. I had a cake mixing bowl and a wooden spoon one year, though I rather liked the plastic handbag that Betty had.

In the holidays, while playing out, Miss Humphries came out with a bag of sweets for us to choose one. I picked out mine and it turned out to be an empty wrapper, I was so upset but never said as I was sure she would think I was being greedy and wanted another, so no sweet for me. This showed my lack of confidence.

It was while out at play that we received our next punishment. A birds nest was found on the ground and we were all questioned to find who had knocked the nest from the tree, I really think it was an act of nature as none of us would ever dream of hurting a nest of baby birds, it wasn't in our nature, however once again we were all given the cane as punishment.

It wasn't long before Geordie was fifteen and old enough to go out to work, we hated to see him leave us, but work on a farm had been found for him. The farm was called Sharnydubs. He was eager to start, knowing in his free time he could go back home to our Mum and Dad.

One Sunday in church we were very shocked when Meg fainted, though Betty thought she was just being dramatic and pretending, she really did feel ill and had to rest before being taken back to the Manse. They thought as she was getting older she needed more privacy and was moved to a room in the older part of the house, I was to share with her for company, I was sorry to have this change but of course I had no choice.

One night Chrissie had been told off for talking after lights out and when caught again she was put into a dark room where she could hear the sounds of a water tank and feel the cobwebs, giving her thoughts of spiders. This ghastly experience left a very serious impression on her and led to her life being spoiled by nightmares. From then on she would scream out in terror, over the years this has caused her much distress. I'm sure that thoughtless deed was not meant to cause such harm.

Mind you, years later I couldn't help but laugh when she told me of a time when her husband Eric was away and she and her daughter Marianne arrived home and saw a bee in their window. They stood outside trying to think how they would cope, both Marianne, and her brother Lee, had a great fear of any insects or spiders, all created by that horrendous punishment. Much more secure in her life now, though never over it, she too can look back and laugh at some of the things created by that night, such as getting a cleaning job in a pub for a short spell, she said "I don't do corners because there might be spiders" – her friendly personality won through to get the job.

Time went on at the Manse and soon it would be Meg's turn to leave school, she was to go and live in Insch till she finished school, then to Aberdeen to attend a two year course in nursery nursing.

Life went on as usual at the Manse for the rest of us, though we knew Mr McMaster wasn't in very good health. This was causing concern but we didn't realise this would have any effect on us. We did feel there were changes on the horizon, especially when Mr McMaster was diagnosed and found to have tuberculosis. This was very serious and made it impossible for us to stay there.

At some time later I woke with a pain in my leg, giving concern to Mrs McMaster. She stood me on a table and was prodding my leg asking for the pain spot, I couldn't tell her, she got cross and gave me a smack, she was worried because of the TB. Thankfully it was nothing much and wore off, but Mr McMaster's illness did mean that once every year from then on we would travel to Aberdeen for a chest X–Ray.

We did wonder where we would have our next home as we were now old enough to worry over this.

Chapter 4

All Change

Once more our lives were about to change, this time life would be very different.

John, Chrissie, Willie and I were taken on the short drive to Insch, only three miles from Culsamond, but new to us. As we were driven through Church Street I saw Meg at an upstairs window, she may have been watching for us, I remember saying 'oh look Meg's got curls'. This impressed me as we all had very straight hair. We never did get the chance to talk to her, instead we were driven round the corner into Church Avenue.

This was to the home of Mrs Vie McWilliams, a widow with three children Sandy, Terry (Theresa) and Charlotte. She chose to have Willie and I live with her, being the older two, as she said that we could help her in the house, I was ten, Willie nine. Chrissie and John, aged eight and seven, would live with Mrs Mary Reid and her husband John. They had three children Gwendy, Phyllis and Geordie. Mary and Vie were close friends so we met Mary in Vie's house.

A box of clothes which we'd never seen before was produced in front of us. I really hated this so much, that moment made a really strong impact on my feelings. The clothes were shared out – this will fit you and so on – I disliked it so much. Mary left with Chrissie and John they lived only three or four doors down on the same avenue.

This was the start of a whole new and different kind of life, I felt sad to have left the Manse and really do believe Mr and Mrs McMaster were sorry to see us leave, however here we were in Insch, our new home. Betty had been driven away we had no idea where to, or why, later we would know it was Aberdeen.

After the Manse the house seemed so small and crowded, it felt very strange and hard to get used to. Gradually we settled to our new routine, I still had a lot to learn – as I found out when I was sent out to buy a loaf of bread. I saw a shop, went in and said 'a loaf please', they all laughed – it was a chemist shop, I was so very embarrassed. It most certainly didn't help my confidence at all, I always felt worried and apprehensive to get it right.

Later when Betty left school she came back to Insch to work in that chemist shop, she lived with Mrs Reid, senior mother of Mary, who Chrissie and John lived with. Meg had been there before and was now in Aberdeen at Nursery College, what a confusing life we lived, even to us!

We now attended Insch school. At least we would now see Chrissie and John in break times. Gradually we settled to our new routine. Vie's was the first house where I heard music played, she loved Slim Whitman records and would often play "My China Doll" and "The Old Rugged Cross", I liked these two songs.

Vie wasn't always very kind to us and Willie and I depended on each other so much for confidence and caring. She would often lash out if anything displeased her. One of these times was while I was making the beds Vie came up to check them, and found a hot water bottle in one. She used it to hit me saying I hadn't made the bed properly. She was a bit like that. Life did have its ups and downs, it was most certainly not all good. I'm sure Chrissie and John had their own issues to deal with in a similar way. Mary's daughter Gwendy was in my class and we were fairly good friends, as long as it was on her terms!

One day Vie kept me off school to look after her as she felt very unwell, although I didn't know it then it was actually because she was losing twin babies. When things got more serious she had me go over and ask Mrs Glennie, her neighbour, to come over. She came and assessed the situation and called an ambulance and Mrs Glennie said I was to go to her house, knock on the back door and ask her son Douglas to make me a sandwich and stay there until she came. Another crushingly embarrassing moment for me! I hated to have to knock and ask. Douglas was a year older than me, he made the sandwich and tea and we sat and chatted, he was so nice. I always held a quiet respect for him from then on.

One treat we did get at Vie's was to go to the village hall and see the film 'Tammy'. This made a big impression on me, I loved it and dreamt of it for weeks, my first ever film.

During the summer holiday the social welfare would hold summer camps, partly to give carers a break and also to provide fun for the children. These would be in schools, usually seaside venues. They were meant to be fun, lots of sport and activities, too much sport for me, and on wet days when the gym wall bars were being taken out I used to cringe. They scared me, I hated them and felt I'd get it wrong and look silly. Making some friends was nice, as were some of our outings to the beach and buying a little gift for our carers.

Our beds were palliasses that we would lay out on the floor, three each, and every morning they would have to be neatly stacked with a blanket and sheet so exactly folded then set on top. This would be inspected daily with marks given for neatness and the best dormitory to gain points and prizes on the last day of camp.

I wasn't really keen on camp, although I suppose some aspects were nice, I was always nervous that I would get things wrong and look silly, though one year I did come second in fancy dress; I used sacks and beads to create the sack look style.

I had sent Vie a postcard and the wording displeased her and she told me she tore it up. One of my friends at camp was to become a lifetime friend, we would keep in touch.

When home and in routine again, I was cleaning in the bedroom and crawled under the bed to get the hot water bottle when I felt a severe pain in my side, I had to stay there till it subsided, it lessened so I never mentioned it again.

That afternoon Vie asked Charlotte and I to go to Drumrossie woods to her Granddad's house with a message. I didn't really like him, I found him creepy as he would try to touch me in a way I disliked, luckily we were never really alone. Still I had no choice so we set off, this visit was okay. The message was for Vie's brother in law as they were now going out with each other. As we made our way home the pain in my side became fierce, I sat down in the wood and wouldn't move. Charlotte was getting so cross and was raging me, but I couldn't move so she had no option but to go and tell her Mum, who got

Mary's husband, John, to come and carry me home where the bed settee was made up for me and the Doctor called. That evening an ambulance was called and I was taken to Aberdeen Infirmary to have an emergency appendix operation. Mary and Vie came in the ambulance with me.

Next morning I woke up in the children's ward and once a little recovered it was nice getting to know the other children on the ward and hearing their stories.

I didn't like visiting time as I had no visitors and would pretend to be asleep. The one day that I did have a visit from Miss Anderson, from the welfare office, I really was asleep and only awake for the last ten minutes or so, but she did bring me some books and a puzzle.

In the evenings Matron would come round with a big jar of dolly mixtures and serve us each a tablespoon of them.

It was on another visiting day that I really did fall asleep and in their well starched and tucked in sheets I had completely turned round in the bed and woke up screaming the ward down. I felt trapped and a nurse came to free me, I was in a panic and claustrophobic. From that day on never again would I have sheets or blankets over my head. I was almost scared to fall asleep.

I was in there three weeks when Miss Anderson came to drive me home to Insch. She had brought in some clothes for me to travel home in and just guessed the size, they were too big and I felt I looked dreadful. I hated them and felt the humiliation of having to walk through the ward past my new friends in those awful clothes, not nice for a twelve year old girl. Later Vie wasn't too pleased to find I'd left my toilet bag behind all because I had wanted to get out quick.

It was some time before I could go back to school and I did note we had a lot of visits from Vie's brother in law. It wasn't long till it was known they were to be married.

One day soon after Vie sat Willie and I down for a chat, she told us we were going to live with a new family. She did say it was only in Church Street at the top of the avenue so she would still see us; she did try to be kind. The person I was sorry to leave was her next door neighbour Mrs Watson who originally came from Belgium. She had taken a liking to me; I would sometimes look after her disabled son Harry for an occasional half hour if she needed to go out with her two daughters. She did say she would have liked to have us but as she wasn't British this was not possible.

It was early evening when we walked up the road to what would be our new home, it did feel very strange and difficult, Willie and I needed each other so much. However, Mr and Mrs Davidson were very kind in their welcome; it was strange for all of us.

We met Helen, who like me was twelve, their youngest of seven, one married and two lived away. It would take us some time to meet and get to know them all. Mrs Davidson had a television, families were just starting to have them, so that was novel for us. They also had a lovely old sheep dog, Flossie, who was grey and white.

In our first week I would see their daughter Elsie sit and sew, embroidering hankies, I was to find out that these were Christmas presents for Willie and I. I thought this was really nice of her. Ethel, a nurse in Aberdeen, would bring us fruit when she came home to visit; I loved the really shiny red apples. This was a very different household from Vie's, Mrs Davidson was much more cultured and there was no more hitting.

Helen and I got along well together; of course she had her own friends.

Mr Davidson was very good in the garden and grew all his own vegetables and potatoes, rhubarb and strawberries. I really loved Mrs Davidson's homemade soups.

I suppose it was only natural that we would have some hurtful and difficult times. Once we were well settled I would notice a strange atmosphere in the mornings when Mrs Davidson would be cold and distant to us. She and Helen would go and lock themselves in the bathroom, it would feel cold, secret and mysterious. I can only think they were making Helen fresh and deodorised for school. Nothing would be said but the atmosphere was unkind and that hurt our sensitive nature and feelings. Willie too felt this. In truth a girl of the same age should have been afforded the same luxury, it served to remind me we didn't really belong.

Every so often Mary and Bunty would come and visit. I didn't feel these visits were much welcomed by Mrs Davidson it made their time with us strained and embarrassing. While in my heart I was delighted to see them, I just didn't have the confidence to be myself. I'm not sure how they were received by Mary Reid when they would visit Chrissie and John on the same day.

At another time there was a school play for the younger children and some of us were chosen to help dress them. It was fun. I so enjoyed it and was delighted when we were given a three penny piece. I ran home excited and proud. Mrs Davidson's face said it all, as I held out my hand to show my coin the icy reply was Helen got home ages ago where have you been? I put that coin down in the kitchen and never touched it again as I felt hurt and humiliated.

There were other times when Mrs Davidson and I were alone that we would sit and chat so nicely, so it was a strange mix, sometimes reminding me I didn't really belong. I was very aware of that and do know and appreciate it was very good of them to have taken us into their home.

Willie and I would have long chats together, he was so important to me as was the love and caring I felt for all my family.

Chrissie was having problems with a really sore leg and would be aware that our local Doctor would try to observe her walking when he thought she was unaware. She sometimes did know as she felt he was hiding behind parked cars to see her. It was decided she would go to Stracathro Hospital. It seemed to us a very long way, none of us were taken to visit her though she was in there for a very long time where she had a major operation and continued her school work while in there. Of course she made lots of new friends. Chrissie had visits from our older brother Colin and met his new wife, Jessie, they lived a bit nearer to the hospital. Sandy was married now too, his wife was called Jean, it would be quite a few years before I would meet them.

When Chrissie finally came home she had a full length calliper on her leg.

I had time off school when I had mumps, spending the first couple of days in bed. Mrs Davidson came up with a cool cup of tea for me and said you might be able to get up for a while this evening, then I spilt my tea. She didn't say too much, but I was so aware of her disapproval. She didn't come up for the rest of the day; of course I didn't get up that evening, after feeling hurt and low all day.

Another difficult time was when friends would ask me "will you come out and play tonight after school". My lack of confidence meant that I hated to ask so I would just say 'no'. I don't feel like it was my own fault but that was how it was, a son or daughter would say 'I'm going out for a while' but it wasn't like that for us. Life is not really so easy and carefree when you are not a family member.

There were times when Mrs Davidson and I would sit and chat. She was telling me she had known our Mum and Dad, older brothers and sisters. Mr Davidson worked on farms for many years and lived in farm houses till he made the move to Insch and now worked for the council road works team.

They still had visits from friends from those days, Mr and Mrs Still would visit and bring fresh milk and farm eggs and her delicious homemade cheese.

Sometimes when visitors came it was not enjoyable for me. I felt in the way, uncomfortable and out of place, so was relieved when the visits were over. Most people would not have any idea of how life can be so different when you don't really belong. This was the fault of our Mum and Dad as I know it was very good of families to have made a place in their home for us.

Of course we had happy times when we had days out and I liked it when we would go to Inverurie to visit Mrs Davidson's Mum and her Aunt next door. We would go to The Dairy, a local café, and have tea and scones. Eventually her Aunt died and her Mum became unable to live on her own so came to live in Insch with us. I always remember the day she came, how she held her precious clock on her lap in the car during the journey. It must have been an ordeal for her.

Grandma was a lovely lady and I enjoyed her stories. She and granddaughter Ethel were very close and, when home, Ethel would sleep with her Grandma while Helen and I had a bed in the same room. I was never asleep very early and I loved listening to their stories together. Other nights I would hear her say her prayers, I thought it was lovely. I never said to anyone that I heard their chats. Many years later I did tell Ethel I had heard and loved the story of her romance with her now husband.

It was sad when Grandma passed away. Mrs Davidson asked us all to go in and touch her hand to lessen any fears of death, it was nice of her when she was grieving for her Mum herself.

Many little chats and touches made me think a lot of Mrs Davidson and I knew one day we could be friends. I know Willie and I would have been less fortunate if we'd stayed with Vie McWilliams.

Her son Robbie had just finished his National Service and had been in Malaya. His trunk was being delivered one day, in it he had presents for everyone, for me it was a brush, comb and mirror set in green with two little cream pots. I was thrilled and thought it was so lovely of him to think of us, it meant a lot to me.

Mrs Davidson's sons weren't always at home as Jim was at university in Aberdeen and Robbie had just finished in army life, so only Charlie lived at home. He worked in the building trade for many years then got tired of being paid off in winter months and changed to working as a porter in a hospital, eventually qualifying to work in the theatre.

Chapter 5

Our School Trip

I was so pleased to know that I was permitted to go on the school trip; this was to be a four day educational trip to Edinburgh. The weeks seemed to pass slowly till it was time for us to set off by coach; I did worry about feeling ill on the journey.

At last the day arrived and I wasn't too bad travelling. We had the most enjoyable time with so much to see and do. The first visit was to Holyrood House with a guide to tell us all of the history. Later that day we visited Edinburgh Castle. Other day trips were to Newburgh Abbey, Dryburgh Abbey and on our last day to Kelso Abbey, after which we were driven just over the border so that we could say that we had been to England. There we visited a gift shop where I bought Mrs Davidson a set of tulip egg cups. We had a wonderful time that I would always remember.

I wasn't really a great scholar though I did enjoy English and loved to write composition. I loved it when we had themed stories and had to write out our own interpretation. I was very proud one day when the teacher said 'I want someone to stand up and read, let's have someone who can read, Alice please read'. This was much to the annoyance of Gwendy who kept pinching me to try to get me to go wrong. I also liked domestic science, our teacher Mrs Gerrard for some reason disliked me and was shocked to find I had achieved a high pass mark in my exam.

At home I made some comment about not being a good scholar and Mrs Davidson said 'you are good at English and do well'. I felt quite proud as this was the only time I had ever heard any comment on any of my school reports or had them discussed with me.

Willie and I were off to summer camp again, I don't think he liked it much either. This would be my last one as I was almost old enough to leave school.

Till then our routine went on as before. On Saturdays I would do the housework while Helen would do the shopping. This was a nice reason for her to go out and chat with all her friends. Willie, too, had his jobs.

Mrs Davidson's daughter Elsie was going to be married, we got to know her future husband Jack quite well. Elsie looked lovely on their wedding day and Helen and I had our hair permed for the first time. It was novel for me to have curls as I had very straight hair. We had nice new coats and hats to wear and everyone enjoyed the day.

Some of my friends were leaving school as jobs came up for them. In October it was my turn; Mrs Urquhart the welfare officer had a job she felt I would enjoy in Aberdeen as a mother's help to a family with four children.

My employers were Mr and Mrs Laing. I would live-in at my work and have every second weekend off when I would go home to Insch.

At fifteen I was very shy, only five foot in height, people thought I was much younger and this was a very different life for me to get used to.

Mr Laing was a restaurateur in the city. Mrs Laing was to continue her career as a Pitman's typing teacher. I would be responsible to help the children get ready for school and in the first months take the youngest to and from nursery and would do the housework. The children Andrew, Ruth, Alison and Valerie were nice children and we got on very well. I was young with them and loved to read them stories, make up stories too, and to spend time with them. I would have an afternoon off in the week if I was working that weekend. It was nice that I was able to go and see my sister Mary who worked in a hostel in Aberdeen. We would sit and chat over cups of tea and her homemade cakes. It was great to see more of her. Once or twice I even went to the afternoon cinema on my own. My wage was one pound ten shillings a week and later went up to one pound fifteen.

When back in Insch I sometimes went to a local dance, which was my only social outing.

After one of my visits to Mary I was on my way home to my work place and stood looking in a shop window when these two lads came and chatted to me, they seemed nice. They said that they were going to buy some chips and asked me to join them. I agreed, but as we walked along one of them grabbed and tried to kiss me; he held me quite firmly till I screamed very loudly. They took fright and thankfully ran off. I made my way home. I never told anyone, I knew how lucky I was and it taught me a good lesson.

Making my way to the bus one weekend, the day was dull and wet. The bus was slowly moving as I went to step on it I missed my footing and fell hard on to the ground. This was seen by two policemen who came to see if I was okay. They wanted my name and address and asked me what school I went to . I was in shock and said Insch before correcting myself and gave my work place. One of them said 'I live near Gordondale Road and will call in.'

I was able to get on the bus, feeling very silly and self-conscious while trying to clean the mud from my coat and my knee. I didn't notice that I had sat next to my ex art teacher Mrs McKenzie, she was very sympathetic and kind, chatting all the way home. I never said how much my side was hurting.

Mrs Laing had not expected to see me on the Sunday night as the policeman had called and said he would call again on Monday which he did. I was pleased to let him see I wasn't the shocked little girl he saw; he was so nice and friendly. I still bear the scar on my side from that accident.

On another bus journey to Aberdeen my brother John was sitting at the back with friends and we waved to each other. I sat near the front and as John got off the driver was chatting to another and said 'that's an awfa fine laddie' 'aye and his brother is too' – meaning Willie. I felt very proud getting off the bus and I felt like saying 'I'm their sister and nice too!' I've never forgotten that, yet because I didn't see them for some time I never did tell them. One day they can read it!

The festive season came and I was invited to Miss Urquhart's Christmas party in Aberdeen, I met up with Sheila who I knew from my days at camp and we renewed our friendship. Sheila invited me to come and stay for a few days when on holiday. She was housekeeper to a widower with three children. Jim was really nice and a couple of years later Sheila and Jim married. I would often either just visit or spend a day or so with them.

Mrs Laing asked me if I would go with her when she took the children for a holiday to The Black Isle, she had hired a cottage for a week. It was a long drive and the cottage was very remote. We enjoyed the days playing out with the children, they loved the freedom, though I did feel Mrs Laing was distressed and in the evenings she would spend a long time on the phone. I hadn't realized she and Mr Laing were having marriage problems.

Some weeks later when I came back from my weekend away Mrs Laing said she wanted to talk, she told me she and Mr Laing were going to have a trial separation. I felt sad for her and wished I had the confidence to say what I felt would be of comfort to her. It was there in my head and heart, I was so young and shy but I did not feel I had the right because of having to keep my thoughts and ideas to myself so many times. I assured her of my support.

It was busy for me in holiday time if Mrs Laing was out and I had all of the children to look after. Andrew and a friend were out in the garden one day when I saw smoke rising above the shed, they had lit a fire! It was small so I put it out and, of course, told them off. Andrew pleaded with me not to tell his Mum, with a firm promise of good behaviour I agreed not to tell, he was mostly a well behaved twelve year old.

It wasn't long before Mr Laing moved back home. He would always come home in the early hours of the morning, I don't know why but he never carried his keys and Mrs Laing never heard him knock, so it was always me who went downstairs to let him in.

Mr and Mrs Laing were going to have a weekend in London, though Mrs Laing worried over leaving the children. I assured her we'd be fine so it was agreed, as long as their Grandfather would call round each evening.

We had a lovely weekend. I spoiled Andrew, Ruth, Alison and Valerie, it was great and we had no problems.

My evenings would be spent in the kitchen ironing – with four children and Mr Laing's white shirts there was always lots. I would just dream as I worked, no one said I had to do this, I just got into the habit. I was quite shy and never sat in the lounge with the family, truthfully I never knew what was expected of me.

A painter, Tom, was hired for some work on the house. Tom was very nice we had many chats at our break time. He was very interested to know all about my work, what I did, my time off and told me of his family and how he played in a group, he loved his music. He said I should visit and meet his family and join them at their club.

What I didn't realise was that Tom Chalmers felt so concerned to see a shy young girl having no fun. He had two daughters of similar age and felt my place of work was wrong for me, although he knew and liked Mr and Mrs Laing and the work was okay. He was right, I did need to be where I would meet and mix with people my own age, I needed this to build confidence; Tom saw that and acted on his thoughts – in other words he cared!

Unknown to me he visited the welfare office to make this known and they agreed and felt a change was right.

It was a shock for me to get a call to say a new job was found for me in the kitchen of a Royal Household. This seemed scary until I reminded myself how many new situations I'd already had to settle into.

I was sad in some ways to leave the children and on leaving day Mr Laing gave me £20.

I spent the weekend in Insch and Miss Urquhart was to meet me Monday evening in Aberdeen; I was booked on an overnight sleeper to London. Mrs Davidson and Helen came to see me off and Tom handed me a small gift of toiletries and asked me to keep in touch. I knew I would keep this promise as I set out on my new venture.

Chapter 6

All Grown Up

It was the morning of May thirteenth 1963 when I arrived at Kings Cross Station and was met by Dorothy, who would take me to my new home. The sun just breaking through and it had the feel of a nice day. I had my first journey on an underground train.

On arrival at Clarence House it was very strange to have a policeman let us in. Dorothy telling me this was the police lodge and at all times the police would let us in and out.

The kitchen staff were sitting having breakfast when I was introduced. Chef Ron Wood-Murray, Margaret his assistant, Dorothy who was a kitchen maid and on the staff kitchen side, Mrs Hards who was to be my boss and Joan her assistant, I would be a kitchen maid. Mrs Hards looked at me and rather alarmingly said 'we'll soon have you lose those rosy cheeks.' I also met May, an elderly lady who peeled all the potatoes on the staff side; Jenny, a cheery lady who kept the floors of the kitchens and corridors clean; and Vie, a proud lady who cleaned in the Royal kitchen. I was to learn of her commitment to high standards she loved to see the shelf of copper pans, now used for display only, looking shiny and pristine. There was a lot for me to take in.

I saw my room briefly when we left my case there before going into the kitchen.

There were two kitchens: Royal and staff. For the staff we would serve around sixty lunches, with perhaps thirty breakfasts, only twenty or so suppers, and very few on duty people would have afternoon teas. It was felt it was better to start work straight away, although I would only work mornings that first week. It passed so quickly, but it did feel really strange with so many people coming and going, I wondered if I'd ever get used to it all. It was Joan who helped me settle into my jobs.

The first morning was over and here I was in the room I would share with Dorothy. It seemed very big compared to the attic bedroom that I had at Mrs Laing's.

The whole top floor of the house was staff rooms; seventeen rooms along two corridors, our room was lovely – right under the flag pole and we had a small balcony. From the big window we looked on to the Mall, St James's Park and could see Parliament and Big Ben. All seemed very grand for a little girl from Insch!

Kitchen staff, housemaids, footmen and pages had rooms on this floor. There was a sewing room and big laundry cupboards along one wall.

This was the home of Queen Elizabeth – the Queen Mother. I will not be making many personal references to the Royal family as it is against the rules and absolutely not what this story is about. While in some ways it must be mentioned, as this was a very big part of my life, but I intend not to break any confidences.

After working mornings only it felt very strange and alien to me being free to do whatever I wanted. A freedom I had never before enjoyed, it took time for all this to register. My life was my own to live in any way I chose.

It took time to settle into my new life getting to know everyone and feel comfortable and confident in my surroundings even going in and out through a police lodge, it was all so new.

Letter writing was to become a big part of my life. I wrote long descriptive letters to people that were special in my life. Mrs Davidson enjoyed hearing about my room the views and meeting everyone, also Tom, my sisters and Sheila. I loved receiving letters. There was a nice desk in our room, I felt very spoiled.

Everyone was very nice to me; I got on well with Joan at work and on her off duty weekends she mostly went to her home in Kent. Mrs Hards took me for walks around the area and another time took me to Epsom to see my sister Meg who was a children's nanny there. Unfortunately someone at the house said she was abroad with the family, we still enjoyed the day looking around Epsom. At another time we went to Greenwich and had a tour on the Cutty Sark. Mrs Hards had known the area as her husband had worked on the waterways. We had lots of interesting conversations together; she was very kind to me. We were again out for a walk when we met her friend Ernest, who walked along with us. He was very nice, though to me seemed rather strange. I was on teas later that day and made some comment to Wilfred, a chauffeur, who gave me some explanation; my first introduction to people who were homosexual. Wilfred was amused at my naivety but I would soon learn that some, but not all, were of the same persuasion in the world of page and footmen and Ernest was a close friend of one of them. I was to learn that he was a very clever and talented man in many ways. He could easily make shirts and suits and was also talented in the kitchen. He worked as butler for The Duke of Bedford for many years. Mrs Hards was good friends with their housekeeper Mrs Cook who I would get to know.

Our housekeeper Miss Jones, a very tall Welsh lady, was very nice to all of us really. Over time I would note the great length she would go to when Christmas shopping to personally chose the right gift for each person from appointed stores, she spent many days at this.

The day we received our gift Miss Jones would stand with The Queen, handing her each gift to be presented. The first year I was very nervous and it went from bad to worse when the corgis jumped up aggressively at me. I didn't know they didn't like people with white coats. In the following years the dogs were not in the drawing room with The Queen and I was able to relax and enjoy the event.

One member of staff became a very good friend of mine, this was Robert McRorie who served meals to the staff and steward's dining room, like me Robert was Scottish. He came from Crieff in Perthshire. Life had been quite hard for him. He was conscious of being short in height and he was fiercely proud of his family. Though very intelligent he had been in service all his working life spending happy years working for Lord and Lady Astor before Clarence House. Robert and I spent many hours sitting chatting in his room, he smoked far too much and liked very strong tea, by choice this would be in a silver teapot and from a white cup, he was very particular about that.

Robert was the only person I was to tell the story of my childhood to, he was very understanding and I liked his version that my mother was undoubtedly a gentle woman, but just a bad manager, saying he knew this by my ways and nature and said it couldn't be otherwise. This was true really as both our parents were actually very intelligent and therefore it was very hard to understand why they had let themselves and their children down so badly. Our mother was an avid reader, I'm told she had been an above average scholar, sadly as often done in those days she had been taken out of school early to work and earn money. The head of the school had visited her father and pleaded to let her continue schooling but was told 'the others had to work so must she.' Our Dad could write such lovely poetry, so both showed a good measure of intelligence.

I gradually grew in confidence and was now finding my own way around and enjoyed shopping in Oxford Street, Regent Street and Piccadilly, and walks in St James and Green Parks. I soon got used to the freedom and making my own choices.

Margaret from Royal kitchen was going to be leaving to get married, she too was Scottish, and took me to her Scottish club a few times. They were more into reels and not so much individual couples. It was fun and I did have a couple of dates with one lad but I didn't go back when Margaret left.

The next one to leave was Dorothy – who wanted to go back home to Scotland. Anne came to take her place and would share my room. Anne was nine years older than me she had come from New Zealand working at different jobs while travelling round Europe. She was so lovely and we became good friends, having some outings together and she took me to meet her Aunt and Uncle. Her Aunt spoiled us so much and made the most delicious waffles with maple syrup. Anne had only a short time with us, six to eight months, till her visa ran out.

Nan was another new staff member for the kitchen. One time a group of us went to the Easter Parade at Battersea Park, it was a great day out, so happy and colourful to see everyone dressed up.

Often we would get together and sit and chat over coffee, this was a new drink for me as I'd never liked it before.

Meg and I would meet up, we enjoyed going to the theatre. The first time for me was to see the Mousetrap, I loved it and many others. We always found lots to do. There was a time or two when we'd arranged to meet that Meg would be late or even didn't turn up – I forgave her because I love her.

As I was travelling staff, my first trip was to be to Birkhall House on the Balmoral Estate.

It was while there Joan and I became firm friends. After our mornings work we would set off for long walks or climbs. Joan was a most delightful companion, I valued her friendship. We came back exhausted, though exhilarated, having to rush to get ready for duty preparing supper.

Birkhall kitchen was full of character with coal fired stoves and three steps leading to a work area overlooking the back door with three cold store larders behind. In one store a specially made wooden stand held a big white milk bowl to hold the milk delivered in churns each day. I loved the charm of it. At the work area Joan and I would prepare the packed lunches for the beaters to take on the hills for the grouse shoot.

Brian the chauffeur would arrive to deliver the fresh bread rolls and butteries each morning, driving at fast speed as near as he could get to the kitchen windows to torment Chef. This vehicle was a brown shooting brake we called 'the buggy' and had originally been driven by the late King. It was a great part of life at Birkhall and in constant use for trips for staff to the village or to Balmoral Castle for the cinema or dances.

Life was so different at Birkhall from our London home. We were a smaller and closer group. Local ladies worked with Mrs Gordon the housekeeper, getting everything ready for our arrival. They were Mrs Syme, Mrs Rose, Mrs Meldrum and Mrs Ellingworth. All were friendly and nice but Mrs Syme was to become special to me. She worked in the kitchen and one of her main tasks was to pluck and clean the grouse. She would sit in the boiler room to do this. Sometimes we'd go in and chat while she worked but soon disappeared when she removed the innards and put them to burn, boy did they smell!

Over the years I got to know Mrs Syme very well. She had four sons and her eldest Tommy was one of a twin. They suffered meningitis at six months old, losing one and leaving Tommy mentally disabled. The boys were all grown up now, but life had been hard for her. They lived in one of four forestry owned houses in the loveliest setting up in the glen, a good walk up from Birkhall. Occasionally Joan and I would walk up in the afternoons and have a cup of tea with Mrs Syme or to June the gardener's house. Her husband and his brother looked after the garden. Chef Ron Wood-Murray was very good to Mrs Syme making sure she had plenty of 'extras' for her larder during our stay. Good job too because if we visited in the evening she would insist that we had some of her homemade soup, even leaving herself short.

I loved my bedroom at Birkhall overlooking the front garden. I would lie and listen to the sound of the water lapping over the stones in the burn that ran through the garden.

In the evenings the staff gathered in the servant's hall where the night sergeant would be on duty. He and some of the lads would play cards while we chatted over coffee. The atmosphere here was unique I loved it and mostly stayed up late before going up the granite stone stairs to our rooms and the lovely cosy feathered quilts. Yes indeed life at Birkhall was special.

All too soon it was back to London, life in the two houses was very different.

Major Anstruther, The Queen's Treasurer, was to pay me what I thought was a great compliment. He had befriended and looked after the life of a family whose father had been his valet/batman during his army career having promised to find a home and work on his own estate in Pittenweem in Scotland when the father's army life was over. He kept his promise and also found work for his daughters. His eldest, Alison, was found work in York House home of the Duke and Duchess of Gloucester. He asked if I would go and introduce myself to Alison as he felt I would be a good influence and provide friendship for her.

I accepted this compliment and went over to York House in Ambassadors Court and introduced myself to Alison, who was strikingly good looking. We sat in their kitchen and chatted over coffee. The next thing was memorable, the gas oven door flew open and all these baked potatoes went flying round the room. We looked on in amazement – Alison had forgotten to prick them. We laughed so much over that. Our friendship was instant and lasting thanks to Major Anstruther we have become lifetime friends and have shared many happy times together.

Life these days was always busy. As well as Alison and Robert's friendship, Terry, one of the Queen's footmen, loved to come to me for chats. Though older than me, Terry had a lot to deal with because of those he worked with. Reg, another Queen's footman, and the now infamous 'Page of the backstairs Billy,' did all they could to make life difficult for Terry so I had a sympathetic ear for him.

In February each year we would travel to Sandringham House in Norfolk for two weeks. My first time there was so memorable, entering the house, walking along a long corridor to meet a maid who truly looked as if she belonged to a century earlier, her black dress, lace apron and strip of lace on her hair set the scene. It seemed unreal and more so going upstairs to a landing where there was a shelf along one wall with a row of filled coal shuttles. Our bedrooms on this landing were so old with iron bedheads and very spooky paintings of war scenes on the walls. The fireplaces, wash basins and jugs, even chamber pots under the beds, all added to the feeling of a past era.

Joan had been before, but Anne and I were astonished, Anne lined up a row of the chamber pots and took photos for her own personal use.

I loved the long walk back along the corridor to the kitchen, which was vast for our small team, and led to a work pantry and another room filled to the ceiling with copper pots of all shapes and sizes. We had to sift through these to find the ones we could use, many were in need of being relined.

That day, as The Queen had not yet arrived, Joan, Anne, Robert and myself were able to have a discreet look around the private rooms and watched a film of the late Queen Mary dressed in her long black coat and hat walking in the garden. This was on a wind up movie film and was fascinating.

At work next day I met our daily help Mrs Green, what a character she was with her Norfolk accent. She loved to gossip and swear after every second word. She gave us many a laugh.

While working Joan and I noticed a very handsome carpenter who rather flirted with Joan though she was spoken for as her boyfriend David was a chauffeur.

In the afternoons we walked around the grounds and the lake or The Queen would ask if the staff would like a trip out and we would have a few hours in Kings Lynn or Hunstanton.

When back in London again Anne was soon to be leaving us, she gave a slide show to let us see the fun she had during her travels, including her treading grapes in France to earn some money, ones she'd taken at Birkhall of us raiding the kitchen at night and the Sandringham ones.

When Sir Winston Churchill died Anne and I went to Westminster Abbey to file past his coffin as he lay in state.

In her last days her Aunt and Uncle gave a small party for her, we had a most enjoyable evening. Mrs Hards and I were there. At the end Anne gave me a very emotional letter to read later, it saying I was the young sister she never had and we must keep in touch.

I loved writing long letters and receiving them, it was a very important part of my life. With Mrs Davidson we became much more like friends and I loved to hear from her.

While at work one day, I went to the silver pantry to talk to Robert when Johnnie, a young footman, came in to put some items back in the silver safe, I had never seen it open before. Johnnie called me in and placed The Queen's priceless tiara on my head and me in my kitchen maid uniform, a lovely moment to treasure. He showed me some of the magnificent treasures in the safe, an amazing collection.

I can't think how it was I came to meet Eileen, I know I was out in the Victoria area most likely sitting having a coffee when we got chatting. Eileen was nanny for Lord and Lady Lucan looking after their baby daughter who was Lady Frances Bingham, to us Frances. Eileen asked if I'd join her one half day a week at a nursery group she attended at Ebury Bridge, we became good friends and spent quite a lot of time together, I think she was rather lonely. She came to London from

Blackpool, leaving her boyfriend and friends behind. I would go with Eileen to their home and was introduced to Lady Lucan who was a very happy young mum. We would sit and have tea in the nursery. Lady Lucan was happy to know her daughter had been on visits to Clarence House with Eileen when she came to see me.

I was in their home one day when Lord Lucan came home. We were all in the nursery, his wife laughingly said to him 'the Doctor has given me the all clear for us to have another baby' a nice tender moment.

Nan invited us to go with her to her Scottish club called 'The Isle of Lewis Club'. We enjoyed it so much that it became a regular Friday night event. I liked the accordion music. The club in Fetter Lane was very small and friendly.

It was always nice to go back to Birkhall, this time for the second half so it would include my first trip to The Castle of Mey. It was nice to see Mrs Syme again. Her son Donald was to become my first boyfriend, friend really as we would go for walks together walking from his house to the glen to the Falls of Muick. We were walking there one day when I thought my eyes had deceived me as I saw Mrs Urquhart drive past us as we walked along holding hands. She didn't stop – not wishing to embarrass me. Some time later she told me she had been on her way to tea with a friend. Other times we would walk into Ballater to the local café where we would play records on the jukebox, these were mostly Jim Reeves records. Mrs Syme encouraged our friendship as she took a very special interest in me. I felt very spoiled by her. Her eldest son Bobby would give people lifts to dances and charge them a small fare price. He never let me pay saying I was Donald's girl. The family were always so good to me. Mrs Syme's husband Tom and Bobby could both sing so beautifully and I'd always think of them when I heard the song 'Danny Boy'.

I loved walking into Ballater in the afternoons, the shops were small and friendly. I liked the gift shops and as it was on Deeside it had plenty of tourists during the season.

The drive to the Castle of Mey was just so lovely. We set off in our sixteen seat bus that we called 'The Grey Lady', taking packed lunches for the long drive and stopping to have them by the Dornoch Firth, I loved the drive.

The Castle was very remote and set on a rugged coastline, it was impressive and had a 'feel' all of its own with the ever present sound of the fog horn making it sort of eerie.

The staff entrance was facing the sea and was normally windy. The very impressive castle door was all metal studded with a big round metal handle. It really gave it importance and was how I would expect a castle to look. This led into a courtyard the entrance to the back.

It seemed out of place to see the kitchen, which was completely modern and didn't have the character of Birkhall. This was certainly not so for the rest of the castle as it was so full of character, the old well-worn stone spiral stairs that led to our bedroom where Mrs Hards and I had communal rooms and shared a turret of the castle as a wardrobe – I loved that!

The walled garden was very impressive it was so nice to walk out each morning and pick the vegetables and herbs, so fresh for use and indeed to breathe in the bracing sea air on the short walk back to the castle.

After our time here we enjoyed the long scenic drive back to Birkhall to finish the season. Our summer season would last from early August, just ahead of the grouse shoot which started on the 12th of August, till after the first week in October, returning to London just after my birthday which was on the 6th of October. The tour would be in two halves: work one, holiday other, changing halves each year always with the same group of staff so I would have Birkhall birthday one year and on holiday next one.

In London it was nice to spend time with Alison. She was telling me she had a boyfriend who was in the Scots Guards and working as an orderly at York House. John was nice and he would often join Alison when visiting me at Clarence House, we all became very good friends.

My room companion was now Pat, a Scots girl, who was engaged to John, a chauffeur. Pat was saving lots of things for her 'bottom drawer'. Robert used to laugh and tease her over this also because she would have a double barrelled name on her marriage. Her name was Lindsay, his Collings, they do sound nice together but this wasn't so, just Robert's teasing.

We still went to the Lewis Club on Fridays.

Joan said she had always wanted to visit the Isle of Skye, so she and I decided we would have a week holiday there at the end of our next Birkhall trip, booking a week in a boarding house in Broadford on the Isle of Skye.

I still enjoyed visits with Eileen so life was always very full.

It was at the club one Friday when these two handsome lads came in all dressed in their kilts and they played the bagpipes for one of the dances. Later one of them came and asked me to dance, this was Rod. We chatted comfortably together, he asked me if I would like to go out with him, I did have to explain that I would be away until October. When I got home I found a little card in my handbag written on it was 'Please get in touch when you get back love Rod' and a kiss.

Once settled in Scotland I wrote to him and we got to know each other by letter, making plans to meet on my return. This was the start of what was to be a fairly long romance.

Rod was a student and in some social groups he would play the bagpipes. Between us we had plenty of functions to attend and had lots of enjoyable times. He came to Clarence House and got to know some of my friends, attending our Clarence House Christmas party and I attended some of his functions. Life was always so full and busy I wonder now how I fitted it all in, enjoying time with Alison, Eileen and Meg, still keeping in touch with friends and family back home.

After we had been going out for some time I had what I thought was a very formal letter from Rod's Mum starting 'Dear Miss Young' and inviting me to spend a weekend. It was a very enjoyable weekend they made me most welcome. Rod's Dad was Scottish and as I came into their home the Andy Stewart record 'Come in come in its nice tae see yae' was playing. This was a lovely welcoming gesture. Over the next two years I had some special times in their company.

Although I had talked with Rod about my Mum and Dad, sisters and brothers I didn't mention the ups and downs of our family life. I didn't feel this was wrong never knowing if our relationship was to be lasting, this was a mistake that would come back to cause me grief later in our relationship.

While again at Birkhall, Joan and I spent the afternoon climbing a hill overlooking Ballater and starting on the fairly long walk back to the house when The Queen's blue Land Rover came to a stop beside us and Don the chauffeur said The Queen would like to give you a lift. We did say 'no' as we felt we looked so ragged with tights all torn by the heather. He assured us we must accept. We climbed in beside The Queen feeling very self-conscious, the lady in waiting and one of the household gentlemen were also there. We were able to explain our 'state' making them laugh, we knew they too had been on the hills for the day's shooting and their picnic lunch. Walking indoors we met Mr Taylor the Steward who thought we'd been attacked, he laughed when we told him we'd just had a lift back with The Queen. It made for a lasting memory for Joan and I.

On another day's walk Billy, a young lad who helped Robert, came with us. We were almost late getting back and had to risk taking a short cut through the front garden. We really never stopped as we worked from early morning until after lunch then straight out just getting back to start preparing supper. After that if the Balmoral dance, which was held every Wednesday at the Castle, was on we would get ready and go to it. 'Oh to be young and have that much energy again!' The next day Joan and I prepared breakfast and Billy came through to collect it. We were very amused to see Billy holding the dish of bacon and eggs standing there asleep on his feet, it was so funny, the poor boy was exhausted.

After this tour it was time for our holiday in Skye. Mrs Symes had asked a relative of hers in Aberdeen to put us up for the night so that we could get our early morning train to Kyle of Lochalsh, where we would get the ferry to the Isle of Skye.

The ferry was very fast I didn't feel we'd moved before we were all getting off.

We very much enjoyed our week in Skye touring round the island, our boarding house in Broadford was very nice, I loved the stunning autumn colours on a tree we could see from the lounge window. The time went much too quickly. We then made our way back to Aberdeen, Joan to go to London then on to her parent's home in Kent while I was able to stay with Sheila, my friend, in Aberdeen, to visit my sister Mary and to see Tom and his family. On this visit Tom had some sad news for me saying that Alison, one of my first employer's daughters, was suffering from throat cancer and no further treatment was possible. It upset me very much. I did visit them, it was nice to see Alison and I was able to play with Ruth, Valerie, and Andrew. Mr and Mrs Laing wanted to know about my life in London and Mr Laing asked how many cars the Queen had. They gave me a lift back to Tom's house. I was pleased that I had made the visit.

Chapter 7

Home in Insch

It was nice to be back home again for the last days of my holiday and to see Willie, John, Chrissie and Betty, when she was not in Aberdeen at work, and to spend time with Mrs Davidson. She liked to hear of life in London.

I went to a couple of dances with Helen, I even had a few dates with a lad I met till I decided I really didn't like his attentions and was pleased to know I'd soon be on my way back to London.

On my return day I would visit Mary till it was time for my overnight sleeper.

It was good to be back and Joan was delighted to tell me that she and David were engaged and would very soon be planning their wedding; Joan asked if I would be a bridesmaid along with David's sister Diane. The wedding was planned very quickly as the day would be tinged with sadness because David was suffering with a life threatening illness.

It was nice to meet Diane and her Mum and make plans to choose our dresses. It was a busy time for Joan. We chose lovely aquamarine coloured dresses for Diane and I. There was a lot to organise. I met Joan's Mum and Dad and they were so lovely.

One day Joan and David had gone shopping in Oxford Street, David said he would go on home as he felt very tired, that day he knocked on my door and I will never forget his handsome face he looked so very exhausted as he said 'Al will you make me a cup of tea?' I was pleased to do this and we sat and chatted as he rested.

Soon it was their special day. Joan's dress was gorgeous, our bouquets were heart shaped and filled with hyacinth giving a lovely perfume. Everything went very well and the day was much enjoyed by everyone.

We waved Joan and David off for a one week honeymoon in Devon. Their week was cut short because while they were walking in the garden David collapsed.

Their new home was in the grounds of Royal Lodge, The Queen's weekend home.

It was a very short time before David's illness became more serious and he was admitted to a London hospital. Joan was given a room at Clarence House so that she could spend the days with David. I went with her one day to visit. By this time he was so ill and it took time for everything to register for him so it was with tears in my eyes I left to get back for my duty. I was just at the ward door when I heard David say 'Al, bye Al' I could hardly see for my tears as I made my way out, only David ever called me Al.

This was in his last days, as only days later I returned from a day out at the Royal Ascot races to the devastating news of David's death. It was heart breaking for Joan, their marriage had been so short.

Many of us from Clarence House attended David's funeral, including most of the Queens household gentlemen, it was a very sad day indeed – full of emotion for so short a life.

Joan was going back with her parents to Kent and of course we would keep in touch.

The relationship between Rod and I continued to flourish. We enjoyed our time together and he would phone when we were apart. Most Fridays we went to the Lewis club to enjoy the dancing.

In May we always had a ten day fishing trip to Birkhall and Chef and Mrs Hards felt I was now able to be left in charge of the staff meals so I would stay at Clarence House. I really was confident in some ways especially in my cooking as I knew the staff liked it better when I was on duty.

I overheard a conversation between Chef and Mrs Hards, a very naughty conversation. They had been given some tins of meat that were dented but they felt were safe to use. I heard the words 'to be sure Alice can use them up while we're on the fishing trip.' That's what they thought but I had no intention of using them.

As soon as they were gone I phoned our butcher and ordered my own choice of meat and disposed of all the dodgy tins. They returned to hear how good the food had been, it served them right, my confidence was growing.

The kitchen staff girls were always changing, also a couple of the younger footmen and housemaids. Although many of the staff were long term and never changed.

I was invited to Rod's house over Christmas that year and again at New Year when we drove to Oxford to see the start of the hunt on Boxing Day, stopping on the way to have a wonderful lunch in a lovely conservatory with friends of his parents. That was a very special day out.

During this year Rod's sister Robena was going to be married and Rod would play the bagpipes for them. It was really nice when Robena called me upstairs to see her lovely dress.

The night before the event with a full house I was to sleep at a neighbour's house and was delighted to hear Rod outside my window whistling 'The Northern Lights' for my benefit.

In the summer time Rod planned his holiday so that he could visit Birkhall, much to the amusement of Terry who handed us our mail each day as I had a post card with one word on it for four days, Here, Now, There, Soon. Of course I knew the reason why, but Terry didn't, he would read them out to the kitchen staff. Rod did come and he travelled with us in the buggy to the Balmoral dance where we had the Jack Sinclair Band play for us every Wednesday during the season. I just can't think where he stayed – it was so long ago it seems unreal.

As always in London, Alison and I would spend time together, her boyfriend John often joining us. Her sister Carol came to work at Clarence House for a fairly short time. She and Alison amused me with their sisterly fights, often over clothes, both were very good looking girls they loved to go dancing at the Lyceum Ballroom and would parade around showing the lovely dresses they had bought.

There was always so much going on; the younger staff members would have get togethers or small parties in their rooms, much to the annoyance of the older staff, as they would last till late at night.

My friend Eileen wanted me to meet her boyfriend George when he came to visit. He very much wanted Eileen to move back to her home in Blackpool. It wasn't long before they became engaged and she was making plans to leave to start planning her wedding, she did ask me if I would travel to Blackpool and be her chief bridesmaid.

Till then Eileen and I would still visit each other, attend the nursery one afternoon a week then on to Lord and Lady Lucan's or Clarence House. I knew I would miss her when she left to go back home.

It was an unusual way of life having all the trips to fit in each year, first Sandringham, then Birkhall in spring, again in summer, and Castle of Mey. It was fun travelling and settling in to different homes where life was just so different and unique in each house. It was the same pattern each year, you soon got used to it and enjoyed the adventure of it all.

It must have been the next Scotland trip while still exchanging letters I got a real shock when Rod said he would come to Scotland and perhaps we could visit my Mum and Dad. Wow, this felt so painful, I felt panicked, how would I handle it – knowing very well how difficult it would be. There was no other way but to write and tell him how my life really had been. The letter was very hard to put together, it would have been much easier to talk face to face. This left me feeling so dishonest realising that I should have told him earlier in our relationship. Had it been a few years later I would have been able to at least take him to meet some of my sisters and brothers. At this time none of them were married or had their own homes so I saw no other way. I knew in my heart I'd handled it very badly and this was most likely the beginning of the end for us.

We continued going out together though as a student Rod had seasonal work at a hotel in Scotland. It wasn't much longer before he came to my room at Clarence House and started a very serious conversation, painful too, saying he had met someone else at the hotel and he felt attracted to her. This girl Christina, was also a student, from Sweden and had returned there to finish her studies. True to my character I quickly said I understood and accepted the situation. Rod asked if I would continue to partner him for functions he had to attend, we could continue to be friends. Of course this was all very painful, although I agreed, and not till I was alone did I try to come to terms with my feelings. It took time to know how I really felt.

We did go out to quite a few events together and continued to chat on the phone. At the beginning of the next year I decided this was not helping me to feel better or sort my life out, so I wrote in reply to one of his invitations saying 'thank you but no, I can't accept as I have to think of myself now.' Rod was very sad and the letter he wrote back said this and that and how he had sat in his car feeling low and miserable. This to me showed he still held some feelings for me and it was of some comfort, so we continued to talk on the phone.

Whether true or not I felt he still cared for me and perhaps the influence of his parents helped him decide to end our relationship, however I would never really know the answer. I must get on with my life as best I can and be glad of the many enjoyable times we had together. I was sad and low for a very long time.

The phone calls helped and when Christina came back from Sweden I met her at the Lewis Club. I showed my strength of character by going over and introducing myself to her in a friendly way while Rod was on the stage playing the bagpipes. I saw him look over and take note of us chatting as did the other band members who had known us as a couple. My friends were all very supportive, Pat was quite funny as we knew Christina worked in a chemists shop in Regent Street, and she went there giving her a look of disapproval even though Pat was a complete stranger, it did make me laugh!

Mrs Symes' son Donald came from Scotland to see if he could rekindle our romance by taking me to Victoria Palace to see the Black and White Minstrel Show. I sat and cried throughout the show as this was never going to happen.

Through going to the Lewis club I did have some dates, none of them really serious. There was Brian the Clarence House electrician, he was a few years older than me and knew of my painful breakup with Rod and I just knew in my heart that he was going to ask me out. I could 'feel' him take interest in me and kept trying to avoid him, poor Brian. He was a really nice guy, nice natured and I liked him as a person but I just knew he wasn't the right boyfriend for me. When alone in the kitchen I hid if I saw him nearby. One day when I was in the storeroom he came in and sure enough he asked me out, if I had said 'yes' I knew he would take it we'd become partners so though I hated to hurt him I had to brave up and say 'thank you Brian but no.' It was very embarrassing, I felt so mean and awful but we got over it, I think he too had endured a broken romance.

Don I also met at the Club, we enjoyed some dates together and I invited him to be my guest when I received an invitation to the Windsor Castle Ball. I made my long dress for this and was pleased with the result.

Alison and John were also invited so we planned to go as a foursome and met in my room first.

After having gone out with Rod for over two years it felt hard to enjoy another boyfriends' company, it was strange though this was a lovely evening which the four of us enjoyed. That evening I got a surprise when The Queen touched me on the shoulder and asked if my partner and I start the dancing off.

'Oh help!' was my thought. Me first on the dance floor – not something I would ever normally have done, Don either I don't think, but of course we did just that both feeling very self-conscious. I bet he hasn't forgotten that, it was a great evening which we all enjoyed. I say evening but it lasted well into the early hours of the morning. As a thank you, Don invited myself and a friend to a party at his house. I can't think who came with me, the night was very strange. In the flat all the walls were covered with silver foil and lots of candles were lit, it was much too dazzling, too much glare with flickering candles. I didn't like it and even more so when I went to go to the ladies and had to go through a bedroom full of floor mattresses – many with couples on them. I hated it and was very relieved when Nigel, a friend of Don's, wanted to leave, asking Don and I and my friend and her partner if we would like to go for a run in his car. That suited me and we all squeezed into his lovely red open top sports car and he drove to Brighton Seafront where we paddled in the sea even if it was after midnight. After this Nigel said he was starving and drove us to an all-night café near Gatwick. We were all amazed at the enormous meal he ordered. The rest of us had more normal meals. This turned out to be such a fun night and it was four A.M. before we got home.

I didn't see Dan many more times. I went out with another boy from the Club whose name was Findlay. I really did like him, he worked in the Royal Bank of Scotland. We went out quite a few times together. I remember he took me to a country folk club and I visited his flat in Forest Gate. I was amused to see his flatmates drinking tea from tin camping mugs. I was sorry to learn he and his friend were going back to Scotland though they did arrange a leaving party first. That night I left the party early as Findlay didn't spend much time with me, leaving me feeling isolated. He did phone to ask me why I had left so we parted on friendly terms. I was sorry he was going as I enjoyed his company, but knew we wouldn't keep in touch.

With Eileen's wedding getting nearer there was plenty to look forward to. She had left Lady Lucan and was back home in Blackpool. For her hen party she had booked a table in the Tower Ballroom. Their wedding day was very special. There was a young lad, one of their guests, who spent a lot of time chatting to me and later said he would come and see me off in my London coach the next day. We exchanged addresses and kept in touch by letter for a time and one weekend he came to London to take me out.

Even now my heart wasn't healed or ready for a new romance and our letters faded out.

Another new staff member to join our kitchen team was Geraldine, who came from Liverpool. She was only sixteen, a great character with a fun personality. I sort of looked after Geraldine, we had fun going out together. Sometime later we decided we'd like to go abroad for a holiday and decided to book with an eighteen to thirty club and chose Italy, a place called Cattolica. We had to save very hard.

The day arrived. As we got off the plane Geraldine said 'the heat from these engines' 'no' I said 'it is the country that is hot.' I knew we would have to take care with the sun. We both had dates on our first day, these Italians don't waste time! They were nice lads, showing us around the area and the best place to enjoy delicious pizza as the hotel food was very poor.

I was very strict to have good behaviour with these lads and made sure Geraldine did too as she could be easily led.

In the next days I had a queasy stomach and my new friend gave me this strong black liquid as a cure, it worked quickly and I was fine. Another day I felt he was getting too amorous so I left him to get back to the hotel, of course me, who had no sense of direction, turned the wrong way. I had to laugh to see my friend sitting on a bench by the hotel. He had waited to see I got home safely, showing himself to be a nice lad.

Geraldine and I booked a day tour to Rome and San Marino, we enjoyed that very much and were back with our 'boyfriends' the next day, I can no longer think of their names, but 'thanks lads, you were great escorts and we loved your company.'

Holiday at an end we went to get our coach to the airport and nearly missed it waiting at the wrong pick up point. We made it though and were sad to leave having enjoyed the most wonderful company, we loved Italy.

We had some holiday time left, so I took Geraldine to Insch with me before Ballater for the second half at Birkhall.

Everyone was saying how good I looked with a sun tan, I felt really good seeing our photos, I was golden brown.

Geraldine wasn't with us very long but we did share some more fun adventures.

As Christmas was near we realised we had no partners to be our guests at the staff party. We came up with what seemed to be a good idea this was to ask two of the guards who we could contact by handing a note to one of them on sentry duty outside the house. We wrote the note asking if he and a friend would like to be our guests if 'yes' please could we arrange to have a night out first?

This was agreed and Geraldine's face said it all as she went up the steps ahead of me. They were not the handsome young lads we had hoped for as escorts. Geraldine wouldn't stop laughing – setting me off while I was trying to smile and show good manners. They hired a taxi, we were going to the Lyceum Ballroom but we could hardly keep a straight face. Once there we escaped to the ladies and were crying with laughter, in truth they were pleasant company. The walk back home didn't help as we noticed one of them had big feet that flapped as he walked setting us off again. It was very funny, we knew they were not the right partners for us, but when they were in uniform and wearing busbys we hardly saw their faces. Very naughty I know, but I phoned them and said the party was cancelled.

This wasn't the last adventure we shared before Geraldine wanted to leave and return to Liverpool. There was a major rugby match at Wembley between Wales and England and a group of the Welsh lads came over to attend. Glen, our footman from Wales, knew some of them and invited them to our staff canteen (bar). Somehow Geraldine and I met some of them who were clearly chatting us up, later inviting us out with them. I did have my reservations about the wisdom of this but they were fun so we agreed, it was a hilarious evening. The two of us didn't drink much but they were in high spirits, one of them continually repeating 'my name is Barry John'. We were told he was a top player. They convinced us to go to the bar of their hotel, we could have soft drinks. I was reluctant as I felt they were married men enjoying a freedom weekend, I felt their intentions and would not let Geraldine out of my sight she was so young and could be easily swayed. I was able to make sure we had a safe evening.

Geraldine did leave to go back home, saying she would come back and visit. She never did but I did have a lovely birthday card emotionally worded saying how well I'd looked after her and much more a lovely keepsake I have to this day from a delightful young girl.

Chapter 8

Family Update

I was now loving the new life I had and this helped me grow in confidence. My sisters and brothers were also happy making, their own choices free from the restrictions we had endured.

Meg was of course in England as a children's nanny, it was nice being able to meet up and enjoy time together. Geordie had his life in farm work, with freedom to go home to Mum and Dad when he could, this being no ordeal for him as he had been away for such a short time unlike the rest of us. Betty, though, still had some restrictions in freedom she was living with a family in Insch and travelling to Aberdeen each day for work in an office. Willie (chose now to be Bill) was doing well in his studies to be a draughtsman. Chrissie (now Chris) was also doing office work in Aberdeen. John had started work in an agricultural machinery firm. Our lives were all changing, Colin and Sandy were in farm work, Mary was a cook in a hostel and Bunty was a housekeeper for two farmers. Not one of us was ever out of work, sisters and brothers who had had so few years with our Mum and Dad each had their own thoughts as to whether or not to ever visit or get in touch with our parents.

Alison and John were planning their wedding; they chose to be married at the Guards Chapel in Wellington Barracks, his regiment's base near to Buckingham Palace, with the reception in assembly rooms above John's local pub. Alison asked her sister Carol and I to be her bridesmaids with her younger sister Barbara as flower girl.

For us we chose strawberry coloured basket weave dresses, so lovely, and Alison's choice of dress was gorgeous.

We all enjoyed a wonderful day, Alison looked stunning, she was a very beautiful looking girl, making John very proud. He wore his guard's uniform. They would then enjoy a few days up North with John's family before starting their married life living in an army barracks in Cheam, Surrey. I missed Alison being just next door, though she came in almost as much to wait with me for John who still worked as an orderly at York House, or I would visit Cheam by train from Victoria Station.

As always it was time for the Scottish trip again. This time with holiday first, where I spent time with Tom and family and some days with Sheila and Jim, then back to Birkhall. This time we would have the Castle of Mey visit.

It was great to see Mrs Syme and family again, everyone else too. Mrs Syme always treated me like someone very special; that meant so much to me.

The journey from Birkhall to the Castle was always a delight. This time The Queen wasn't arriving until the next day so we had time to settle in.

Nan was another young person with me, she had found out there was a dance in Thurso that night. This was a five or six mile journey from Mey, we had no problem to get a lift there but no transport back. We still went and enjoyed the evening and had to chat up the local policeman to give us a lift back. We were fairly sure being the Castle that he would say 'yes', but he also said that we must wait till the hall was clear of people, then he would drive us home. We thanked him as he left us at the top of the drive.

It was very dark, windy and eerie with the foghorn continuously sounding. We had forgotten that with The Queen not in residence the night sergeant would not be on duty, so we'd have to wake June the housekeeper to let us in. It was so dark, Nan was desperate for a 'wee', we did laugh as we made our way to the back courtyard where we knocked for June. She took ages to come and wasn't too pleased with us as this was around 2am. After letting us in through her quarters to the servant's hall she locked her door behind her. We were starving and while waiting for June had planned we would raid the kitchen for some eats. We put the kettle on and made to go to the kitchen for milk and eats but we couldn't get the door to open it was firmly stuck. We were both tired, it was very funny really. With no food we were lucky when we looked in some high cupboards and found some blankets and cushions so we slept on the floor as best we could.

Poor Robert when he came in next morning got such a shock to see us there and we noted he hadn't unlocked the door, just firmly pushed it and it opened. We laughed so much and made our way to our rooms to get ready for work – me crumpling my bed so that Mrs Hards wouldn't think I'd been out all night! Nan and I never told anyone of our adventure.

While working in the kitchen here we overlooked the front and could see The Queen and guests out playing croquet or The Queen walking her dogs.

Nan had an on-off friendship with Johnnie – one of the young footmen, though I knew she held ambitions to be an air hostess and was making enquiries in that area.

Chapter 9

Holyrood House

The Queen was going to be on a four day visit to Edinburgh and we were going too. I was so delighted to know we would live and work in Holyrood House, that to me felt like a very special treat. Having visited there as a girl, never did I ever dream I would actually sleep there!

I loved this visit – everything about it thrilled me, even if we did get off to a bad start with Chef getting cross with us. Having arrived first he expected the kitchen stores to be unpacked and stored. We got over this and once settled Mrs Hards and I went for a walk along the Royal Mile later in the evening. We then sat in the servants hall hearing ghost stories of earlier life at the Castle, a bit spooky in such an ancient building, but I was fine. Nothing spoiled my enthusiasm for being here.

In my room there was some crested note paper and I made sure I wrote to friends. On the next day we visited the Castle, I loved the whole experience of those few days. Mrs Hards and I enjoyed a walk around the gardens to see the flower clock. It was a very busy few days with so much to do and see – we wanted to fit a lot in and yes we did fit in some time for work as well, having lived in what I think of as the Palace of Holyrood House pleased me very much indeed.

Another Scottish girl joined our staff, this was Greta. She and Nan became good friends and went out a lot together. Greta worked with me in the staff kitchen. She was a bit older than me and we enjoyed a great friendship. Mrs Hards considered making Greta up to assistant cook as she was older, I was fuming over this to such an extent I went to Chef and very firmly let it be known. I had been doing the job for much longer and had been left sole responsibility many times, I should therefore have the promotion. We were very nervous and laughing with fear when Chef called Mrs Hards to his office telling her I was being made her assistant. As she returned fuming banging her fist on the side table Greta turned in shock holding some tomatoes now behind her back, they plopped into the sink of washing up water, giving us the giggles. Greta didn't want the assistant's job so it caused no friction between us. Mrs Hards said I won't teach you, I won't help you. This was ridiculous really as I had been doing the job for so long already, I was always doing the breakfasts on my own Mrs Hards was usually so different to her outburst and always said if you ever need any help let me know, she and I got on really well together and were a good team.

Nan was lucky in her application and was leaving for training at Gatwick, her job as an air hostess was to be with British Caledonian. She was delighted to be working her notice and we were sad as we were out on my room balcony to wave her off.

This wasn't to be my room for much longer as Miss Jones, our housekeeper, said I was to have my own room now and let me choose new wallpaper. This had been Joan's, then Nan's room.

Speaking of Joan, we were always in touch. She eventually met Max who was twenty years older, they married and had a lovely baby girl, Emma. Joan asked me to be Emma's godmother, I was delighted, she was a gorgeous baby.

I was sorry to have left the big room but it was nice to have my own room. I was now at the side of the house facing Lancaster House and could still see onto the Mall.

Greta and I had so much fun and laughter together sometimes at Mrs Hards; at the amount of ingredients she put into her stew, or the 'adventure of the day'. She made steak and kidney puddings once and had them all set up ready the day before they were needed to find by the next day they had soured and smelt so bad that she couldn't use any of them, wicked I know but we did find it funny to see her trotting along the corridor to the waste area with bowls covered with tea towels. Or she used to make jugs of gravy to last a few days and if there was some left on my weekend on she would say 'Alice you can use this gravy', no way, I hated that and tipped it away to make fresh. One of the reasons they liked it better when I was on duty.

Robert and I always worked the same weekend, he used to get up to all sorts wanting to make tablet like his mother used to make and set about this. It turned out different every time either too hard or toffee like and stuck. It was a caper. Sadly I didn't know the recipe. We enjoyed the more relaxed weekends as Royal staff weren't working, they mostly had weekends off as they worked later week nights to prepare dinner whereas we worked every second weekend.

Robert loved a laugh he was a great character, his laughs often at the expense of Billy and Reg – some of the footmen who he had no time for because of their various antics. Robert knew them all very well indeed.

One of these antics was to affect me, as I was in bed one night and at 1am a neatly cuffed hand pushed someone into my room. The door opening had made me look up to see what it was, I shot out of bed, I had a very drunk chauffeur in my room. David was new to his job, he was a very good looking young man, who was married and his wife was only weeks away from having their first baby. He had returned from driving Billy Tallon, the page, back from Windsor where Billy had been on duty with The Queen at Royal Lodge. Once back, Billy invited him to his room and plied him with drink, no doubt with very dishonourable intentions. When this didn't go his way Billy had no hesitation getting rid of him to my room – off his hands not caring how I dealt with him. I tried to get him to leave, even offering him coffee to sober him up, but he was too drunk. I phoned the police lodge, he followed me out and was sick along the corridor which I felt obliged to clean up. I was telling Bridget, a housemaid, next day. She confirmed 'yes that would have been Billy'. Horrid person, there was plenty of mean tricks that were his fault especially to Terry. He and Reg made Terry's life quite miserable, they were quite a pair.

That year at Birkhall Greta and I continued to have fun, like the time I came up from the kitchen to see her pour away juice from the last tin of fruit she had opened. I said that Mrs Hards uses those and in a panic she filled them up with water. We had a hard time to keep a straight face when Mrs Hards did come up and say I love the juice for my fruit salad. We never let on and got away with it. There were many funny stories.

We were amused to know our Chef had a lady in his life, she was also called Greta. Chef had been a widower for many years; he had two grown up daughters and some grandchildren. This kept him in a great mood he and Terry always had lots of banter together. We really did have some great fun such as the day we stood in the kitchen, it must have been an arrival day for us, when Mrs Hards stepped out of the buggy looking a bit stylish in a dipped hat. Terry, Chef and I were in the kitchen Terry says 'Oh my here comes Chicago Lil' it was very amusing. It would be impossible to capture in writing all the hilarious incidents that happened over the years.

In London we had Pat and John's wedding to look forward to. Greta and I were asked to be Pat's bridesmaids and Alison had asked her if she would like to wear her wedding dress. Greta and I chose green dresses, however we found them a bit straight to walk in. Pat had been very lucky as Mr Maurice, The Queen's hair dresser, had been at Birkhall and heard of Pat's wedding and offered to come and dress her hair for her special day. The November day was the coldest ever. We had to put rugs on the heaters to warm them and then wrap them around ourselves so that we weren't shivering for the photos. In spite of that Pat looked lovely and we all enjoyed the day. I was getting to be an expert at being a bridesmaid – this was my fourth time!

Pat and John were moving into a flat in Marlborough House Mews.

Next we had to think of our dresses for our staff Christmas party and we decided we would make them ourselves. Neither of us were experts so it was a big chance and Greta's wasn't finished on the party day. However, she was very lucky as Glen, a footman, had a friend, Ernest, who heard of this, he really was an expert we were amazed when he took that dress apart and remade it on that day and she wore it that night. He was really very clever and saved the day.

Greta wanted to leave and go back into nursing as she had done in Scotland. This time she wanted to train as a state registered nurse and was lucky to gain a placement at St.

Thomas' Hospital so would be nearby and could often call in to visit.

One of the biggest changes in the kitchen was with Chef, who was going to retire. He and Greta had bought a house on a hillside in Braemar, he loved Scotland. This was going to be a very different life for him from his London home in Golders Green.

Our new chef was Michael Sealey he was very different from our last chef. It seemed really strange at first. Michael had worked with a team of chefs at Buckingham Palace and was now ready to be Chef for The Queen Mother.

We all settled into being a new team, though we continued to have staff changes and now were joined by two girls from Canada, Sandra and Maggie. They were on a work permit so their stay wouldn't be very long. They were both really nice girls.

When the time came for the Sandringham trip I was going as staff cook with Sandra to help me.

Sandringham had been undergoing major renovations to modernise the staff bedrooms. I felt this was a shame as it had lost some of its character. We now had a new purpose built bedroom block above the kitchens. I missed the feel of the walk along the long corridor to our olden style bedrooms and back to the kitchen. Of course much of the house was still the same. The kitchen was vast for our small team. We still had to rummage through the copper pot store to choose pots we could use. I loved the feel of the place and it was here Sandra and I became firm friends. We worked well together and spent lots of time in either of our bedrooms chatting and getting to know each other. I was telling her of my first Sandringham visit and how she would have been fascinated with the charm of it.

As it was February and often very cold we would each go and have a sleep in the afternoons. When not going out this day I woke with such a start thinking I'd slept in. I dressed, ran to the kitchen and trayed up the bacon putting it under the grill as Sandra came in. I realised it was supper I should have been starting, that put me out of sorts. Sandra and I laughed over that. The trip was great fun and everyone gave Sandra and I great praise for the standard of the meals served. We were really pleased at that. We still had Kate Green as our kitchen help, as always she was very funny. I'm not sure Sandra understood her Norfolk accent. As we left I told her I would bring a swear box next time and she would have no wages left.

At Clarence House Sandra continued to come in for coffee and chats to my room after our work. I knew I would feel very sad when she and Maggie left for Canada. I knew we would always remain friends even if I doubted we would ever meet again, but life is full of surprises.

Alison now had a young son, Alan, and was having a second baby. We continued to spend lots of time together. Sometimes John called in for coffee in the afternoons so we always kept in close touch. One time they left after a visit and John rushed back to collect Alison's handbag which she had left behind. We were amused to hear that while running through Green Park he had been stopped by the police because he had the handbag under his arm. His explanation assured all was in order and of course there was no problem.

There was a new young housemaid, Margaret. She was from North Wales and her Uncle was one of our three orderlies. These were army men posted to Royal Households for duties such as seeing to distributing the post, attending to requests from the five Gentlemen of the Household, and the Master of the Household, Lord Adam Gordon. I'm sure they had many tasks. Robert liked Margaret she enjoyed having a laugh. I can think of some very funny times we had. I remember her laughter one day when Robert brought her up some cheese on toast, the cheese had been left from the Stewards Room lunch, this time it was blue cheese. Margaret hated the smell of the hot cheese. Little snatches, just so many of them.

As I was walking back through St. James Street one day Helen, who was a new dresser for The Queen, caught up with me, introduced herself and said 'actually you and I are sort of related.' We had cousins married to each other she said. She asked me if I would like to come to her room for coffee. I hadn't visited rooms on The Queen's floor before as Miss Suckling the dresser whose job Helen took over had just retired and while she was pleasant enough she felt superior in her ways. I thought she was until I saw her with too much drink one day and noted the 'real' person but she and Miss Field kept themselves apart.

It wasn't the same for Helen, she was young and full of fun, enjoying having young people around her.

In London we didn't often sit in the servants hall, but one night a group of us were in there quite late all sitting chatting when well after midnight John Leishman, a footman, said he was starving and wanted us to go out for an early morning breakfast at the very smart Kensington Palace Hotel. So we hired two taxis and did that. It was great fun, we had such a good time and it was 4am when we got back.

The only sort of scandal I got myself involved in was caused by Alison's John. I had been out for dinner with Margaret (housemaid). We had enjoyed a lovely meal at her Uncle's in Reigate and as we came back we could hear people in the canteen. I heard John's voice and had an idea he would think he would come in for coffee, but as it was already very late so I locked my door and went to bed. I did hear the handle turn and ignored it knowing it would be John it never crossed my mind how much he must have been drinking. He got the idea that he could take a short cut to Ambassadors Court by climbing through the fire door over Clarence House roof to reach there and of course was spotted by the on duty guard caught and held by the police. He was really very silly to have done this crazy thing. Of course this news became a big scandal with everyone gossiping. Margaret sent word for me to come up to her room at break time as she heard of the goings on. I felt guilty because if I'd just let John in this would most likely never have happened. Mr Sumner the Queen's detective questioned me to get my account, he was a friend. I hated to have him question me, however there was nothing I could do. The result of this was that John lost his York House posting and was returned to his regiment, and as Margaret told me was being posted to Sharza in the Persian Gulf. I felt awful for Alison as this was to be an unaccompanied posting and she would remain in married quarters in the U.K.

Of course Alison and I chatted over this event but remained firm friends; she continued to visit me and I to visit her. She now had two boys Alan and David and now lived at army quarters in Brookwood Surrey. Only Alison could ever have got away with how she used to phone me and say 'Alice I'm coming to visit, I've got no money can you meet me at Victoria Station and pay my fare.' I'd never have dared to take such a risk. Alison just gave them her winning smile and got off with it. Her good looks always won through for her. I expect I would have been arrested there and then.

Helen was a great addition to our group of friends, she soon got to know Greta, Pat and Alison. Helen was a great seamstress and started to hold sewing and knitting sessions in her room. We all enjoyed these times together, not Alison of course as she had two young boys. John was away with the regiment so we still had lots of time together. I always think of us somehow saying 'we'd meet at Trafalgar Square'. One day when we met there a very young Alan saw me and darted between these two policemen saying 'mind there's my Auntie Alice!'

A group of us planned to go to Spain for a holiday though we were lucky in as much as Helen had a friend who was happy to let her have use of a flat in Spain for two weeks. We really needed to have some spending money. Our living accommodation was excellent but wages were not very high so we had to think of some ways to earn some extra money. There was about six of us going and we were to be joined by a couple of lads that Helen knew from Scotland. We managed to get some extra work as chambermaids at the Strand Palace Hotel, not much fun really but it did help us save for holiday money. We did find work we much preferred, which was occasional work for Searcys agency serving food for cocktail parties and dinners. I did like the cocktail parties, not so much the dinners as I was much too nervous. I had a nightmare once at the Cumberland Hotel. We were serving a major dinner party – this wasn't the kind of event I liked, and it was not good for my confidence especially as I kept running out of food. Both the first and second course ran out before I got to my eighth guest at the round tables. Though not correct I thought last course I'd start at the other end and serve them first, it was so different at the cocktail parties and buffets, I enjoyed those. It was at one of those parties in Millionaires Row, Kensington that I served our then Prime Minister, Ted Heath. We worked for some time at that agency. I had made my own black dress as part of the uniform. We still continued meeting up in Helen's room for our weekly sewing sessions or just fun and chats.

Chapter 10

Family Wedding

It was nice to hear that Chris and Betty planned to share a flat in Aberdeen. Though Betty was in her twenties, the family she lived with in Insch were rather hostile on hearing this news. She really needed to do this for her own confidence and freedom. She and Chris loved their flat share and being able to invite Bill or John whenever they wanted, as well as to see Mary who still worked in a hostel.

Whenever I was in Aberdeen I always called in to visit Mary as did the rest of my family. In some ways it felt as if our family was divided in two parts, those who had been taken away from home and those who had never left, it was through Mary it seemed we all came together and be reunited as of course we had spent many years apart.

I'm not sure how long Betty and Chris were in the flat before Betty met the man she would eventually marry, Brian. He had spent some years in the merchant navy before finding work in Inverurie locomotive works. We were delighted when the time came to know they were making plans to marry.

I was over the moon to hear from Bill that he and his friend Gordon planned to come to visit me in London. They found a place to stay at a Salvation Army Hostel. I had to make a firm promise not to tell any of their friends that they stayed there! It was lovely to see them; we had a lovely few days together and I can picture Bill now as he walked away from me on an underground escalator. To have him say 'I love you' just stays in my heart as a precious memory, to see and know the kind soft and emotional side of all my family always meant so much to me.

On my next holiday home, chatting to Mary and Betty created a big ordeal for me as I was going to go to Bunty's work with her in the farm house then going to go to our Mum and

Dad's. This felt very strange indeed for me and I cannot describe, even now, my feelings on this visit. Was I a stranger? Was I family? Who knows! If I'd been bolder in confidence I could and should have asked some questions, but no, I couldn't. They were very nice and seemed pleased to see me. My Dad talked kindly saying how worried he'd been when I was very young and had to be rushed to hospital with diphtheria, having to be fed through a tube in my leg and in danger of losing my life for some days. That weekend I met Jean, Sandy's wife for the first time.

The time came for our holiday in Spain. The flat was on the outskirts of Benidorm. The group of us who were going out included Brenda, Helen, Greta and I. We had saved very hard and to save money carried our own coffee, sugar and butter. I really don't know how we got off with it. I'm sure we wouldn't have these days. The immigration officer tested the sugar and he gave us no hassle. I think Helen's sister was joining us with the lads from Scotland. The flat was lovely and again it was a really nice holiday. We had trips into Benidorm and walks round the orange and lemon groves. I think my holiday in Italy beat this one, but it was still really nice and a great holiday.

Soon it was time for Betty's wedding. This was going to be in Insch Parish Church. I so much looked forward to this as it was a special family time, always precious to all of us. Betty looked lovely for her special day and at the reception when the minister made his speech I thought it was very moving as he gave very great praise to the Young family of their excellent reputation throughout the village. Of course I loved it, though I could see Bill and John cringe at so much mention though I'm sure he too felt pride. Chris did as we talked about it. This was a very enjoyable day, that is till late evening as John left the hall and crossed the road and was hit by a car. Before we even knew it he was being rushed to hospital in Aberdeen where it was discovered that he had two broken legs. He was very seriously ill.

I was staying at Mrs Davidson's. The next day Gwendy, my friend, who Chris and John had lived with, came to ask if I wanted to go into Aberdeen with her to see John. I so wanted to but could sense Mrs Davidson didn't want me to. I know it was silly but I still had confidence hang ups and always worried about displeasing. As it was I was going the next day on my way back to London and I would visit John then while in Aberdeen.

The night of the accident I did go down to Mary's house to wait for news of John and knew he was seriously ill but hanging in there. I was very upset and concerned for him. Mrs Davidson didn't like Mary Reid and I knew she didn't approve of me going to their house, but that night I needed to do that to find out about John and to me Mary was always pleasant and sociable.

I did see John the next day it was very upsetting especially knowing that I had to go back to London. His mouth was very dry and uncomfortable but he said a few words to me and I left feeling very sad and tearful promising I'd write and keep in touch. He was in hospital a long time but thankfully made a full recovery.

I walked through Ambassadors Court so many times either to go to Oxford and Regent Street shops or to visit Pat at Marlborough House Mews. She now had her young son Peter. I always seemed to meet with The Duke of Kent and so many times he used to say hello to me.

I had an amusing incident one day while walking there with Pat's son, Peter, who was around three. One of our Clarence House daily ladies caught up with me, she was a real cockney talking lady, but this day was making a strong attempt to talk nicely, sounding 'all posh', very strange. She shook hands with an astounded Peter. I was amused when I realised that she had somehow thought I was looking after the Duke's son Freddie, who was the same age and same colouring. I never told her different. It was very funny leaving her to feel she'd shaken hands with the Duke's son

We loved having small dinners or reasons for get togethers on quiet weekends and I planned to have a Burn's supper for some friends, having Helen involved. It grew to be a much bigger event as she invited a group of Buckingham Palace staff. We went to a great effort to make this an enjoyable evening and it really was fun. So many people came that we had to ask Miss Jones if we could hold it in the staff recreation room.

I had no boyfriends in my life at this time though I somehow got talked into going on a blind date with a lad who worked on The Royal Yacht. He wanted a partner to use some tickets he had for a last night at the proms concert at the Royal Albert Hall. Bill Bridle, one of our police lodge team, took it upon himself to introduce us when Chris called for me. It was a great night out. The next day Chris took me aboard the yacht for a look around before going out to eat, so the whole weekend was a real thrill. They were only there for a few days so I never did see him again.

Margaret was going to be leaving as she had met Eddie and they were going to be married. She wanted me to visit her family in Neath with her and she would tell her parents of her plans. We had a very special few days, her parents were so lovely and her Dad took a real shine to me. They took me on lots of sightseeing trips, I felt very spoiled by them. They planned to come to London for Margaret and Eddie's registry office wedding. On her last week we arranged to go out for a meal, a group of young girls, to The Blue Boar Inn in Leicester Square, this was a hen party for Margaret. We had such an amazing night – the young waiters flirting with us, it really was a most enjoyable night out.

Theresa was the new housemaid to take Margaret's place. Though a little bit older than us she fitted in very well with our group, happy to join Helen's get togethers or sit and chat in any of our rooms. Terry and Robert often made appearances to torment us. I spent a lot of time with Terry helping him with his Christmas shopping as he used to spend so much money buying presents for the family he made his home with. I had the marathon task of wrapping all his and mine. Terry and I were quite good friends, he thought a lot of my friendship always telling everyone 'whoever marries Alice will be a very lucky person!' He said that so many times and it was a great compliment, even if I did sometimes wonder if I would ever meet the man I would marry, perhaps one day, who knows?

Meg now had a young daughter, Celia, and she was working in a nursery with their home in the flat above. It was nice to go and visit them or have them come to me. Celia was a very beautiful little girl; I loved her little sayings especially when

Meg asked if she wanted a fried egg 'no Mummy' says Celia 'you make them rusty round the edge'!

I still spent a lot of time with Alison and her boys, Alan and David, they were constant visitors to me though John was soon to finish his tour and would be back home, they were then moving to Germany with the regiment.

I also spent lots of time with Pat at Marlborough House; she was having her second baby.

Betty and Brian had now moved from Scotland to Swindon for Brian's work and they had a new baby son Gordon. It was nice having them in England so I could visit them more.

There was always my letter writing which I spent so much time on. I loved writing long letters and of course receiving them. Mrs Davidson and I became good friends through our letters, I loved hearing from her, also Sheila, Tom, Sandra, Anne, and Joan. Mr Taylor our steward used to always say 'if you want to know how anyone is ask Alice, she keeps in touch with them all!' Indeed I did as much as possible.

Joan was now a busy Mum with her second baby son Andrew. She and Max had made their home in Ashford, Kent. Joan had come to visit when Emma was small. At that time she had said she would love to be at one of our staff Christmas parties where she would see so many old friends so I was pleased to invite her as my guest and Mrs Jones said she could stay overnight. The Queen was pleased to chat with her and to remember David, she liked to see faces she knew.

Another time my sister Chris came to visit and Mrs Jones was happy to let her stay in an empty room though, being Chris, in the middle of the night she came through to share my bed saying she was worried there might be spiders in there. She hadn't changed, I loved having her and showing her round. She was then going on to Swindon to stay with Betty and Brian and little Gordon our gorgeous nephew.

Other visitors I enjoyed were Mrs Syme her son Bobby and his wife Betty. It was a wonderful visit after a sad family time for them.

We visited the Post Office Tower, it was fairly new then. We had much laughter with Mrs Syme who was scared of the height.

We were so sad to hear that Mrs Syme's husband Tom was diagnosed with terminal cancer and only a very short time later lost his battle for life. The family were all so nice I never forgot how special Mrs Syme made me feel, so I wrote a letter of sympathy. It got back to me that on receiving my letter she said 'ah this is the letter I've been waiting for.' Having been told that meant so much to me and I loved spending time with them when they came to London once a little recovered.

I got to hear of an agency in need of baby sitters in a high class area and decided to apply. I had some interviews and was pleased to be accepted, it was good to make some extra money and my idea was that if the children settled I could write some letters.

One of our kitchen team, Brenda, had planned a 21st birthday party in Bracknell. Chef, Maggie and I were being given a lift with people we hadn't met. Chef was fairly shy so I had to get a conversation going, we couldn't sit in silence. Later Chef thanked me saying 'I was glad you were there'. It was a great evening and we had a good time. Helen was there too, as she had been at Royal Lodge she had no problem getting there.

Helen, Brenda and I each made our long dresses for that night.

Chapter 11

Fun Events

I was now in my twenties and well settled in my life, feeling I'd earned my place as an important and worthy member of staff. This was good for my confidence. I had many friends and was never short of things to do.

Life within the household followed the same pattern each year. In February the two weeks at Sandringham, a ten day fishing trip at Birkhall in May and at Birkhall again in August for the grouse shoot. For us, we stayed into October though Balmoral's season ended in August at the end of the tour travelling to the Castle of Mey for two weeks before a last week at Birkhall.

The week of Royal Ascot we were lucky at Clarence House to each be invited to enjoy a day at the races with a badge for entry to the Royal enclosure. As part of the staff kitchen team we had the task of making up the packed lunch boxes for each day's group. It created much excitement, choosing our outfit which must include a hat. It was nice seeing everyone's choice of outfit for their day. It was an exciting day out and a break from our everyday routine.

When it came to the day for any of the kitchen staff there was much excitement to get our outfit right as any staff member, once dressed in our special attire, presented themselves to the kitchen to show off their chosen outfit. This was very important as to gain entry to the Royal enclosure hats must be worn. It was always fun shopping for a special outfit, not the everyday clothes we would wear. It was special to be given this experience and we felt very spoiled being on the Queen Mum's staff. We travelled there in the grey lady, our coach, lunch boxes on board and felt so lucky compared to the general public as the traffic and parking was a nightmare. We simply made for the Royal enclosure car park and had much less of a problem, often being more spoiled by the gentry who knew our coach and often offered us champagne and strawberries. It was great being part of it all, I loved it and it pleases me now, all these years later, to think of it and to have had invitations to so many major events, always in good seats, such as Wimbledon tennis, not for me this one, The Royal Tournament at Earls Court, and The Garter Service in Windsor which I enjoyed very much indeed. Little did I realise that one day Windsor would be my home.

There were other functions we got tickets for if we wanted to attend, The Beating of the Retreat and the Trooping of the Colour. There were tickets we could use if off duty, always in first class seats. Most 'Troopings' I was working and the Queen liked us to go into the garden and watch the procession while looking over the hedge. She always gave a special wave to her staff as they passed, as did most of the Royals. It was wonderful to have been part of it all so many times over the years to feel I'd touched on, known and been part of some of these prestigious events. Even now, when I see Jeremy Kyle on television, it reminds me of those days when he was a very young boy. He came in on those days with his parents as his father, Mr Patrick Kyle, worked in our wages office where I had to sign to collect my money on pay days.

There was also the Royal Tournament at Earls Court and sometimes tickets for a cinema previewing and one or two theatre tickets. One time or another I had enjoyed all of these as well as entry tickets for the Ideal Home Exhibition. I felt privileged to have enjoyed all these times that I would otherwise have had no part of.

Here at Clarence House we were always kept busy and with so many people passing through it was little wonder it took me some time to get used to it all in those early years, from the regular visits of Mr Potter, attending clocks throughout the house, Joan the telephone cleaning lady, Mr Maurice the Queen's hairdresser, Mr Norman Hartnell the Queen's dressmaker and his two lady assistants, one known as Miss Evelyn who was model for the Queen's clothes. Both Mr Hartnell and Mr Maurice were so lovely to get to know over the years, working on the ground floor you get to meet everyone. Our daily driver delivering the bakery items, a never forgotten face as he became so ill with flu one day. Jenny and I were shocked at his appearance saying 'he must have time off'. The next morning we were very shocked to learn Mr Harris had passed away during the night, that year many died in a flu epidemic. We were very sad as we made a collection for his family.

We had some laughs too over our "book in for meals" system. Mrs Hards was sometimes over strict when meals were taken but not booked. There were one or two real upsets caused over this. Terry used to make fun of the upsets except if he was on the receiving end!

I was enjoying my babysitting evenings and meeting some really nice people. These were mostly in very grand houses or sometimes hotel rooms.

After the child or children were settled I sat and caught up with my letter writing, mostly long and detailed, often describing my surroundings. One in particular was like a dream house where I sat in the loveliest kitchen diner. The units were all white with plum coloured doors, an amazing breakfast bar and a dining side which had white seating around a white table which had a bowl of orchids in the centre. Right opposite was a white grand piano, it was very luxurious. Sometimes the clients were most interesting. There was a Doctor and family in Harley Street who had two young children. The mother loved my way with the children and on a second visit asked if I would be interested to come and work for her. There was a top composer at a hotel babysitting job, whose son I minded. At Whitehall I babysat for politicians' babies, that was nice and near home and, very naughty I know, I used some of their headed notepaper for a letter. I'm sure this would have been for my friends Sheila and Jim in Aberdeen as Jim was a keen philatelist and also collected crested paper headings.

An American couple had started to ask the agency if I was free to babysit for them. I got to know them quite well, spending occasional days minding their four year old son. His mother was having her second baby. I took him to Clarence House one day and he enjoyed seeing the guards on duty. When I wasn't working I helped where I could especially when the mother went into hospital to have her baby. It was on one of those days her husband came home and insisted I stay for supper. I can't even think of their names now. He was a lovely man, though it concerned me a bit to accept. He insisted I stay and try a proper homemade American burger. I was a little nervous to see the dining table all set with a nice salad for the two of us and some nice music playing then inviting me to the lounge for coffee. It really was so innocent and very nice though seemed a bit strange. He even gave me two records to keep. They had their new daughter. I did sit for them some more times and always wondered if he told his wife he had me stay for dinner! They were leaving to go back to America after the mother asked me to show her how to make Yorkshire puddings.

There was one fairly sad babysitting I did for an eleven-year-old boy called Jasper. I remember his name. His Mum explained to me that he was having a hard time coming to terms with the loss of his Daddy who had recently died from cancer. This was her first night out since then. Jasper was a lovely boy. We sat on the stairs him talking of his Daddy, he asked if I would like to come and see some of the carpentry items he had made for him. I was pleased to do this though seeing one almost finished item was so emotional. I found it hard to keep myself in check. I felt proud to think that chat may have helped him. His Mum wasn't late and poured us a both a sherry and we sat and chatted. I could never forget this lovely family.

There was another babysit request that left me astonished as I knew the address was that of Lady Lucan. I had been to her home many times years before, this was now after the dreadful events of 1974. I have to confess I was a bit apprehensive. Lady Lucan answered the door and knew me immediately saying to come in. She chatted to me about Eileen, her first nanny, and I asked how Francis was. That was fine though she rather strangely said 'I'm sorry I'm not going out now' so of course I left and decided I'd go and see Pat at Marlborough House and tell her of this astounding coincidence and my nearly babysit. I was really quite glad, it would have felt strange being there knowing the history. I most certainly wouldn't have gone down to their basement kitchen to make tea.

It was so strange for that babysit to come up. I'd have to remember to tell Alison of that when I wrote as she knew Mrs.

Maxwell-Scott who was the Duchess of Gloucester's Lady in Waiting and who Lord Lucan had visited that dreadful night.

There was just so much to my years at Clarence House getting it all in and more or less in the order has been quite a task and with so many new friends both coming and going over the years. If they had all stayed as long as I had it would have been easier!

One other adventure I had enjoyed while Geraldine was still with us was our meeting with two soldiers while they were on duty at Balmoral. We had some good times together. We used to go for most enjoyable walks and climbs up the Craigendarrach Hill, it was so much fun, or we'd meet up in Ballater and go into the café and play music or attend local dances. I can remember us still dancing on the fairly long walk back to Birkhall, the lads walking us back even though they had to walk back after. Oh to be that young and fit again! Both were called John one had a nickname Penny as his surname was Coyne. They were nice lads and they planned they would come to London last leave before their tour of Northern Ireland. This was in the early years of the renewed conflict. They did come and stay at army accommodation at Waterloo and we had some fun days out in London and a night at a bierkellar in the Strand. It was a very hot October and we spent time sitting in St James's Park promising to write while they were in Ireland.

'My' John was keen to make our friendship more serious, I wouldn't agree to more than friendship, but we did write to them.

Geraldine's John wrote a letter to me, it was quite emotional, asking of Geraldine's commitment to him saying he would respect my opinions as he felt I had a soothing effect on him and he held me in much respect, spoiled only a bit by him saying soothing effect like his mother and me in my early twenties! I think there was a compliment in there somewhere! I could not fail to mention these lads as we enjoyed their company even though we eventually lost touch once they were back home in Scotland. Indeed John Willoughby and John Coyne were nice young lads it was a pleasure to have known them.

I can't think why it was that I was asked to work at Royal Lodge one weekend to cook for the staff. I do remember I was not very pleased about it that time, though once there I enjoyed it very much. I was able to look around the house and lovely grounds , also having a look into the Dolls House. I had been there once or twice on visits but it was nice to see it properly. It was there I met Mary Elizabeth, she was really very lonely as Miss Anthony and Mary her assistants weren't really very kind to her. After that weekend I promised I'd visit Mary as I chose to call her as her second name was used only because there were two Mary's in the kitchen. I kept that promise and travelled to Egham to meet up with her a few times. It wasn't that long before she wanted to go back home to her family in Aberdeen, where she soon met the man she wanted to marry and asked if I would be her bridesmaid, promising to choose a date when I'd be on holiday before going to Birkhall. I was pleased to accept and again wore the dress I had for Joan's wedding. A year or so later Mary became the proud mother of twin boys. She was happy to be home nearer to her family and I expect she was kept so busy that we did eventually lose touch.

Another memorable one-off event was one year when our Sandringham trip came up and there was still so much renovation ongoing that the Queen accepted an invitation from her friend, Lady Ruth Fermoy, to use her Norfolk home for that year. Lady Fermoy was also one of the Queen's Ladies in Waiting. This was agreed, but a smaller amount of staff would be needed, some of us arriving the day before the Queen. The kitchen was really nice with a lovely red Aga to cook on. It was only to be Chef and I, he was joining us the next day. Once settled in Mary Doran (the housemaid) and I went for a walk around the beautiful grounds. That night I made them steak, chips and salad and Billy Tallon led us all into the delightful drawing room. I think he rather thought he was Lord of the Manor as he served us all drinks! It really was a most enjoyable evening and we felt very grand. Lady Fermoy's granddaughter was Lady Diana Spencer. It was very nice to enjoy those days in her lovely home and we all enjoyed it very much indeed. Then it was back to London for normal routine.

Some nice news from back home was to hear that my sister Chris was going to be married. Her future husband was in the Royal Navy and his base was at Rosyth where they would start their married life. It was nice hearing all her news of how her plans were developing; the wedding was going to be in Insch in March. I most certainly would be home for that again. It was a lovely wedding, Chris looking so lovely and so happy we all enjoyed the day. It was nice to have a few days home to see everyone again.

As time went on there were other family weddings. One that was a big surprise to us all was my sister Mary, who was in her late thirties, she had decided to say 'yes' to Willie who had so wanted to marry her many years before. I had never known of this, she kept saying "no" so she and Willie had a quiet registry office wedding in Aberdeen. She continued to work at the hostel. Willie had already retired as he was quite a bit older than Mary, perhaps the reason she was so hesitant. She and Bunty had always been constant company for each other so it would be very different for her now, though of course she was a constant visitor and they could still have some time together.

Pat was pleased to find a job that fitted the hours she wanted, this was doing housework in a flat nice and near to home for Mr. and Mrs. Manning, a Jewish couple, who owned a hat making business. They sometimes held function evenings where Pat was involved with serving and one time when they were having a cocktail evening Pat asked if I would join her as a helper, this was not through the agency. We really enjoyed the evening and Mr. and Mrs. Manning were generous with our payment. Pat also had another part-time cleaning job in Berkeley Square for Mrs. Black and they had a baby daughter and sometimes needed a babysitter. I filled in for Pat for that job one night. On arrival I almost bumped into Ronnie Corbett coming from the house next door. He was very nice as he said a few words to me. That night as I sat watching an Alfred Hitchcock film all was quiet and just as someone was creeping down a stair in the film the net curtain in the room I was in flew over my head. It made me scream and my heart beat faster I got such a fright! I had to go and check the baby, she was fine, still fast asleep. Pat and I also served at one of their cocktail parties.

We had such fun that night and Mrs. Black was a superb cook, her food was wonderful. For dessert she made the most scrumptious meringue tower. Pat and I were so well thought of that some of the guests wanted to hire us for their parties. However, we could not tie ourselves to that as we had our own work. It really was enjoyable.

Life was really that busy I was never ever short of things to do or friends to visit.

Once more it was holiday time before our Birkhall trip. It was nice to be back in Scotland to visit with my family and friends. Like me, my brother Bill suffered the pain of a broken romance so I was pleased to know he was happy again in a new romance. Some time back he and John had been involved in a car accident, a friend of theirs, the son of a local policeman, had been driving and the car had left the road tumbled down a bank stopping by a small burn. Bill had to pull John from the burn as he was dazed, it was very scary, though thankfully all three were okay when over the shock.

At Birkhall we settled in again. Terry told me that while working in the upstairs work area the Queen would watch us working away, I expect intrigued by all the goings on.

One afternoon while alone in the kitchen the Queen came in – she had been fishing and held a salmon which she had caught and asked me to weigh it. I could hardly even hold it especially once it was hooked on the hand held scales, it was so heavy and slippery. I had visions of it landing on the floor. The Queen and I, both not that tall, struggled to hold it, luckily Mr. Pearl, her ghillie, came to our rescue.

Helen and I were at a local dance in Ballater when we met Brian who chatted to us for much of the evening and said he'd give us a lift home after which he did. We thought no more of it until the next afternoon when he arrived at the door in his butler's uniform, holding in his hand an old pair of flat scruffy shoes, very embarrassing because they were my comfy ones I used to change into for the walk home to Birkhall. I had left them behind. I cringed as I collected them and thanked him. He then asked if I would like to meet up with him the next evening. I agreed and we had a pleasant enough evening. After that he asked if I would like to have coffee at his work place as it was on my way home. I was pleased as I knew he worked at the home of the Johnnie Walker family. The drive had always left me curious when I'd walked past, as you couldn't see the house from the drive. We had coffee in the kitchen, Brian went out for a few minutes and came back with five roses that he had picked for me. He couldn't show me round as the family were in residence. Over the next few days Brian declared that he loved me which gave me an instant dislike for him. He became a nuisance and kept bringing me presents. I did tell him but he seemed to take no notice. I was very thankful when his family were closing their Scottish home ahead of us and he would leave with them. I made sure no addresses were exchanged though did worry he may know the Queen's London home but luckily that was the end of that.

Once again we were on our way to the Castle of Mey. I always so loved the journey, the scenery was magnificent. I'm sure it wasn't always sunny but it lightened my heart and felt like it.

We enjoyed our time at the castle. If we arrived ahead of the Queen, Robert and I liked to look around the private rooms and the dining room with the elaborate crested fireplace.

I know some of her guests had the same idea, as I found out one afternoon. I was sitting on my bed in my petticoat enjoying a quiet read when the door burst open and in came Princess Alexandra and following her, her husband Angus Ogilvie put his head round the door. They were most apologetic saying they were having a look around the castle. All I could do was stay there and smile! I was telling Mrs Hards saying "I don't know who got the bigger shock them or me"! It was very funny really and makes for a good memory. I often used to pass some of the Queens guests on the spiral staircase. At the end of the castle tour the Queen's family were spending time on the Royal Yacht and liked to sail as near to the Castle as they dared to give a noisy salute to their mother. For this event the Queen wanted us all outdoors to help create a noisy welcome return salute. Joan can vouch for this as in her time with us her Mum and Dad had come to visit. Joan was most embarrassed with her Dad creating serious noise hooting the horn of his car. She need not have worried, that's what the Queen wanted, to make our crowd heard by the Royals on the yacht. It was very funny, the noise was enormous and then we waved them off before going back to work. This happened on most of the Castle trips – the horn on the yacht sounding a few times in salute.

While at the Castle Mrs Hards and I used to have a half hour walk after we had served breakfast. We used to sit on the Queen's bench overlooking the sea, seeing the seals bobbing about on the water. This was very pleasant before going back to the kitchen.

Chapter 12

Birkhall Party

This year near the end of our Birkhall season the Queen was to hold a party for her staff. This would be in our recreation hut and she had asked the Jack Sinclair Band to play for us. Billy made some fancy drinks for us and I only had one drink. It either must have been very strong or had something extra added. I found I really let my hair down and enjoyed a wonderful evening. I knew I was much too open and chatty, telling everyone how special they were to me. I was totally extrovert and danced nonstop. It was very strange at the end I felt light headed and ill. I was sure that drink was specially mixed by Billy, did he want me to make a fool of myself? If so, it had the opposite effect and actually left me feeling that everyone seemed endeared to me. Chef made me laugh as I think it was the only time I was ever late in the kitchen and looking ill! He laughed saying "oh Alice you are a real person after all," whatever that meant, I did wonder.

Work really was very hard to get through that morning but I made it and would just have a sleep in the afternoon.

It was nice to be in Aberdeen early on the day of our return to London as then I could visit Mary and Willie. This day Mary was busy making oatcakes and I was eating them, so delicious freshly baked, along with Mary's endless cups of tea as she kept topping them up. Mary was one of the most good natured people ever, her healthy rosy cheeks and happy face made her really special. She loved to have any of the family visit her. Willie loved to joke, he and Mary were so happy together.

I left to get my overnight sleeper train and back to the London routine. The non-travelling staff were glad to have the house reopened again.

Lord Adam Gordon had now retired. Our new Master of the Household was Captain Alastair Aird though, as a close friend of the Queen, Lord Adam was often a guest.

Settled in London and everyone was getting together again visiting Pat, Greta calling in, seeing Helen as we were on opposite halves.

Greta had a new boyfriend. This was Lucky, he was from Ceylon as it was then. He had a flat in Gloucester Terrace and, like us, he and Greta liked to hold small dinner parties so we had many fun evenings together. His sister Rosy was going to be married and Greta asked if I would do the wedding buffet. I asked Chef if I could use the kitchen, which he agreed to. Helen and Greta were pleased to help. We had a great afternoon in the royal kitchen preparing all the food and loved joining them at Lucky's flat later. Mind you we got a taste of Lucky's dreadful driving as he drove us, transporting the food. Rosie was so beautiful and dainty in her sari.

There was one of the major celebrations for the Queen at Buckingham Palace when all the public had gathered along the Mall and crowded the palace gates. Terry and I had been out somewhere and came back passing there. Terry had a good sense of humour, he had me crying with laughter as the two of us stood outside the palace gates because Terry saw the Queen, indeed all the Royals, many days as his work as a Queen's footman meant he had close contact with them. This day he stood with the crowd shouting with them "we want the Queen" and telling the nearest listeners "I've come all the way from Bournemouth to see the Queen." It was very funny, we then walked back into Clarence House. We really did have some fun.

There were serious times too of course as one day I went to Robert's room to find him feeling rather ill and he didn't want to fuss, saying he'd just rest. I left him feeling unsettled and was lucky I went back as I could see he was in real distress and felt sure it could be a heart attack so I called the police lodge. The nurse and an ambulance came. Even though he was ill Robert was quite proud and said 'I'm not leaving by the back door'. A quick word with Miss Jones and it was agreed that he could be taken out the front door. He went into St. Thomas's Hospital. Thankfully Robert came through this. When I visited him in hospital he insisted that I had saved his life. He was going to be away for some time and I knew I would miss him; he went home to his flat in Crieff to recover.

There was great excitement with a very important party the Queen was holding here at Clarence House. Chef told us all not to make any plans as we would all be on duty. We spent hours getting all the preparation done – it was great fun we loved doing it, there was a great buzz about the house with so many people on duty. There was to be a 2am breakfast on offer and it was after 3am before we finished that night, I loved those one off events.

Not so much though did I like it when the Queen's nephew, Lord Elphinstone, used to visit, often arriving after 1am, and it was me that the on duty footman used to come to. I used to come down to the kitchen in my dressing gown to make marmalade sandwiches for him, he was diabetic, and this was his request. I did this quite a lot of times over the years and always in the early hours of the morning. My easy going nature led me to be woken up for this. As I didn't work on the royal side it really wasn't my job.

I was pleased when Robert was back with us. They were going to hire someone to share his duties. This was Norman Brown an Aberdonian, I liked Norman though I don't think Robert was too keen. Mrs Hards liked Norman too; there was a real friendship developing between them. Norman was a widower in his late sixties and Mrs Hards was five or six years younger. Norman drove a red mini and they enjoyed going out on trips together. Robert was teasing over a budding romance, not knowing how true this would turn out to be.

Soon it was time for the Christmas party – always fun to go and choose a new evening dress. I was pleased with my choice of a deep purple velvet dress with a white lace bib style front. The reaction I got that evening was a bit special for me, I didn't realise this till the next day; I was never the glamour girl, I felt, not having the height for real style. Of course, I was young and proud of my nice clear skin and could look and feel nice. I was proud that night to have so many compliments. Even the Queen's Lady in Waiting asked me 'where did you get that most enviable dress?' Captain Aird's wife and many others made a point of making comment on my dress, I hadn't realised I'd chosen a dress so right for me and with my hair dressed in a put up creation the way I liked, it was flattering to know I'd made such an impression. Added to this, the next day I was told of Danny, one of our orderlies, having said wasn't Alice very glamorous last night, wow, me! This was new to me and I still feel cross that I never had a photograph of that night in the dress I hadn't realised was so special.

Robert invited me to spend a few days in his flat in Crieff and asked to see if Greta could join me. He was very proud of his home and loved showing me little items he had bought through Miss Jones, he had a keen eye for antiques. We accepted his offer and loved Crieff. We met his sister Bunty. Greta and I planned to cook a special dinner for the four of us. Robert worried over us getting out all his best china dinner service, we assured him we would put it all away correctly. We had to borrow some cooking dishes from Bunty, it was a super evening, an absolute delight to share his home and have such a happy evening, Bunty loved it and Robert loved to be entertained in his own home. I knew then Robert thought of me as a true friend; so very few people would have been welcomed to his very private home life. Robert was a very proud man, he loved his family dearly helping where he could to fund the schooling of his nephews, Bunty's two sons. One was training to be a vet, the other was training in pharmacy. Perthshire was beautiful; one of my favourite counties for delightful scenery and Crieff would always be special to me.

Robert wasn't too keen on work at Birkhall as we were all in too close proximity, unlike at Clarence House, and the servant's hall where we worked was always full of people, so he had no space. For the footmen the hours were long they had to work hard looking after guests coming in and out, they were amused at us younger ones finding it such fun. We also worked longer hours and no days off with first Chef, but Michael changed that insisting that we each have a half day once a week, he much preferred London. He was often very funny, one day seeing a ray of sunshine on the steps he shocked us all diving down saying "sun, I must touch it", he did make us laugh.

Indeed we could not have had two chefs that were more different, each nice in their own way. At the time of Wood-Murray I was just a young girl much too shy and quiet though felt glad for him to have seen me come out of my shell a bit. Now as an adult I could interact more, I had my own voice and was respected and thought of as sensible and well behaved. This was important to me.

Again it was time on our half for the Castle of Mey. This time the young policeman who came each day was really nice. I felt flattered that he seemed attracted to me and I was therefore delighted when a night out at a lounge bar in Thurso was being arranged for a group of us. The policeman said he would join us, it was a great night. We did sit and chat together, I felt sad that we were travelling back to Birkhall the next day, so nothing could come of it.

This time, I was sorry to know it had been arranged that I would travel back with Pat's husband John in the Queen's Jaguar, fancy, sorry to travel in such style but I so liked the slower journey in the 'grey lady', mind you I felt very grand in the Queen's car and we did stop off at a nice restaurant in Bonar Bridge in the most glorious setting. Of course the journey was much faster, I decided, yes, this was a bit special.

I don't know if it was that evening but I know I did have to prepare a light meal for the Queen one night at Birkhall and Mr Taylor said the Queen couldn't have had a better meal, so I felt very proud.

At the end of our Birkhall tour the Queen was again having a recreation room party for the staff with the Jack Sinclair band playing for us. Later some of us met in the servants hall for tea or coffee. Jack and his band joined us, it was very sociable and nice, of course we were in no hurry to leave. The atmosphere changed when Mr Taylor came in ranting, telling the band to get off home we have all the clearing up to do – he was really nasty. I was incensed and lost my cool at him, giving him such a dressing down for his rudeness right there in front of everyone, he was dumbstruck with shock. I said the Queen would be horrified with his behaviour after having invited them to play for us on her behalf.

There was a big silence, I just felt it really needed to be said. I don't think anyone would have ever believed I'd done that and spoken up to Mr Taylor. I knew I was right, the Queen had invited them, I knew she would expect them to be looked after. As he had said "we have all got to clear up after you" I added 'since when do you ever clear up after anyone, everyone else does it?' Jack was astounded as he'd known me over the years and I had always been quiet and said little whenever he had seen me, but he truly deserved it, I hated rudeness. In truth I think Mr Taylor was very hurt to have the mild mannered Alice turn on him. I actually liked Mr Taylor but too much drink played a big part in his behaviour. He didn't speak to me for some days after until one evening we sat in the servant's hall and he came over handing me two train warrants for our return to London saying I'll leave these with you Alice for safekeeping. This was his way of making peace with me, as he'd done wrong and I'm sure the incident had upset him. We were 'friends' again from then on.

It was only one lad and I going back on that sleeper – I really don't remember his name now as he only stayed in royal service a short time. He didn't know Aberdeen and we had a few hours to fill so I invited him to join me visiting my friends Sheila and Jim. I'm sure they were thinking he was a boyfriend of mine but this wasn't so. Jim went out for fish and chips and we enjoyed a pleasant few hours before having to leave to get the train. It was a bit strange having a lad with me as we couldn't sit and chat too long, each having our own sleeper. I never did sleep much on these, though comfortable enough, I was always awake to see all the different stations the train stopped at.

One of the times I was paying my own fare and chose to have a reserved seat. It turned out to be a memorable night as I got chatting to a lad of around my age, it was nice to pass a few hours, we even went through to the refreshment carriage for a while. All was fine until he said 'can I ask you something but please don't laugh,' intrigued I said "okay I promise". He then said "will you marry me? I do have a life to offer you as I work on my father's sheep farm which will be mine one day" What did I do, I laughed, saying "don't be ridiculous we have only just met and don't even know each other". From then on I couldn't wait for Edinburgh where he was having to change trains. I couldn't believe he'd asked me that so seriously. Had anyone else told me they had been proposed to in such a way I doubt I would believe them, but it can happen.

Chapter 13

Special Invitation

I had now worked for ten years at Clarence house and was almost twenty six. Jenny, one of our team, must have started the same year. I hadn't realised this until we both received an invitation to the Queen's Buckingham Palace garden party, it was nice to go together. This would mean another new outfit to include a hat. I was pleased to find a lovely dress that felt very smart and would be my next Ascot outfit.

It was a lovely day at the garden party, Jenny and I enjoyed it very much and felt ourselves very grand as we walked along the Mall and into the Palace gates. It was nice to have the tourists look on wondering who we were in level of importance, it was a very nice day to remember.

There was another important occasion I could wear this outfit, as my brother Bill and fiancée Jackie were planning to be married.

I would most certainly travel to Scotland for that and very much looked forward to the day. It was nice to hear news of their plans. This was to be in Aberdeen, as anytime we had family functions it was always special for so many of us to be together.

Jackie looked very beautiful and was a welcome happy addition to our family. We were only sorry Chris had to miss this day as she was in hospital in Rosyth where she gave birth to her second baby, a son Lee, brother for Marianne.

At one time I stayed in Rosyth with Chris for a few days. Marianne was a gorgeous little girl. It gave Chris and I time to chat over our younger years and thoughts and feelings. We each had different incidents and hurtful times to put up with and always the question, why was it allowed to happen? We never really understood, we can't imagine what our parents' thoughts and feelings were when they went home to a much reduced household, it must have felt very strange, were they upset? We would never really know. At any time when I have been with any of my sisters and brothers we have talked of this. Why our lives were so completely changed by these events we will always wonder. It would remain a question none of us would get an answer to.

Alison and John were soon to return from Germany and would be back in Brookwood, Surrey. They now had four sons: Alan, David, Stephen and Peter. It would be nice to have them back home. Alison's Dad now worked for Sir Ralph Anstruther and came in for a meal sometimes as his chauffeur.

We were still having staff changes in the kitchen and Mrs Hards had asked her friend Wyn to work with us. This had not been a good idea as they were soon falling out. I had been away in Scotland and came back on the early train to find Wyn doing breakfasts on her own as I always did, this was a nightmare. The porridge was boiling over, toast burning in the grill and she was trying to cope with the eggs in the pan having put too many in at once.

I had to help her out not even going up to change, later that day she left without saying to anyone. That was the end of their friendship.

I sat in with Mrs Hards catching up with the news, she was telling me she and Norman wanted to marry and surprised me saying that she first had to divorce her husband as though estranged for many years they had never divorced.

She and I always got along very well together. I never forgot how kind she had been showing me around when I was first in London.

Norman was now over seventy this would be a big step for them, she added she was thinking about when she would retire.

The group of us younger girls continued to have get togethers – mostly in Helen's room. We had some real laughs and capers like the time Sheila, the laundry maid, came in after she had been at church then the pub! She was a bit 'worse for wear'. Terry was in too and teasing her saying she was straight laced. For some reason she thought to prove this was not the case she stripped naked. She was very funny she was quite a character.

At Christmas that year about six of us received an invitation to Princess Margaret's cocktail party at Kensington Palace. Billy and Reg were also going and wanted us to have a drink in Billy's room before leaving. Though I was always wary of them it was fine. The party was lovely, Princess Margaret was just so welcoming and charming as she came to chat with each of us, she was a great hostess. Her broadcaster friend Derek Hart was her companion that night. Seeing her reminded me of the time she came to stay at Birkhall. She brought her new dog, a Dalmatian, with her and sent a letter to me, this was her menu for her dog. We laughed over this three-times-a-day menu it seemed very strange for a dog!

Mrs Syme gave up her Birkhall work, she had now moved into a house in Ballater since losing Tom and worked at the café. I visited her there and at her home and she was now thinking of moving to Irvine in Ayrshire to be nearer her son, Bobby. I knew I would miss her but would always keep in touch.

I still spent plenty of time on my letter writing and liked the reactions of my friends when they received them, one saying 'I love your letter and like to take it on the bus to read on my way to work'. Another 'I make a coffee, sit, relax and read'. Sandra in Canada loved to receive my letters.

Other special memories, also from times at Birkhall, must surely be the Ghillies' Ball, which was held at the end of the season at Balmoral, and nice to have chosen our evening dress for the occasion. This was attended by all the Royals in residence I couldn't fail to notice the Queen's photographer cousin Patrick Litchfield so full of life and vitality as he rushed round taking many photos so it seemed sad to see in later years how he had changed, having remembered how when at the Castle of Mey him introducing us to his new wife.

In the early years I attended the Ghillies' Ball while dancing the 'Paul Jones' and the music stopped with me opposite Prince Phillip. I was very young and nervous as we danced together though managed to chat with him. The next day Chef said he was impressed at my confidence dancing with the Prince.

Over the years Prince Phillip got to know my face at Balmoral. I was most astonished some years later when he said to me 'hello, how is your Dad?' I was stunned till I realised who he was mixing me up with – one of the daughters of Mr Anderson, his Balmoral farm manager. I knew the girls as two worked as students at Birkhall. I was amused to feel he must think me the plain one of the family as his girls were all very glamorous though I did share the same hair colouring and very fair skin.

In a little way it felt quite flattering. On realising his thought I did have the courage to tell him of his mistake and he laughed.

Another memorable moment was having seen Prince Andrew when he was just over three. He and his baby brother Prince Edward came to the kitchen windows one day when I was working alone in the kitchen. The windows being half below ground level they were kneeling down looking in, I was very amused at this young Prince saying to me 'what is that miraculous spoon you are using?' This in fact was only a straining spoon. Having seen glimpses of him over the years and while at a fancy dress dance for the staff Prince Andrew was to pick out the winner. As I saw a fifteen year old eye up a girl in a very short skirt it made me think of the tiny boy at the window and to know why the Queen had his valet accompany him to see that he didn't get in any trouble the valet telling us later, it was an amusing moment.

At these events we had a dance every Wednesday at the Castle with the Jack Sinclair Band to play for us, for the Ghillies' Ball we had different bands, Joe Loss or Jimmy Shand or Ian Powrie. It was nice to feel that we had danced to all the major band groups, I loved that thought.

Sometimes there was a film show at Balmoral, the Royals sitting at the front, the benches at the back which the staff would sit on were leather covered and filled with coarse hair padding and I learned to take a cardigan to sit on as they could be very prickly. One of the films we saw was Tom Jones. It was very amusing and caused great laughter for both the staff and Royals when the film broke down at a critical moment.

In our household, whether at Sandringham, Birkhall or the Castle of Mey, The Queen very often used to say to the chauffeur "would the staff like to have an afternoon trip out today?" and this would be arranged. At the castle there was a good choice of outings to Thurso or Wick or the Caithness glass factory or John O Groats or Duncansby Head. One time the Queen, wanting to treat us to tea, arranged for us to deliver a book to a relative making sure they had tea for the staff, all much enjoyed times over the years. Once at Birkhall an invitation was received for the staff to visit Glamis Castle, that was very nice, a lovely tea was laid on. Even Robert and Mary Doran came that day! It was much enjoyed and we didn't have to rush back as the Queen was away on an engagement; that was a really nice outing.

Indeed we were spoiled – I would not imagine the much larger Palace staff would have such treatment.

Another Castle of Mey memory from my earlier years was being there when the very first Mey Highland Games was being organised – or, well... sort of! It was a hilarious scene, they had invited the Queen and when the time for her arrival came nothing was underway, no games or competitions started, so they insisted we start a tug of war between the Castle staff and locals. I was roped into that, pleading was how most events got underway. It was so funny. By the next time I was back, two years later, the event was much more established and became an annual ritual. While there, there was a sheep dog trial and a local dance in the evening. This was great fun in such a small place and it was after one of these dances when Billy, our page, got himself in some bother. He had been attracted to, and tried chatting up, a local lad resulting in this young farm worker being greatly offended and chasing Billy round the village and Billy having to knock on the door of Mrs Waters who at that time worked at the Castle. She had to take him in for protection, of course this caused much hilarity. That dance was given the name 'Sheep Dip Shake' by some of the amused footmen.

The Queen was a very proud lady, this pride leading her to remove a bandage that had only that day been put on her leg. Her physiotherapist had joined us at the Castle to dress her ulcerated leg and as we all were at Scrabster to see the Queen launch a new lifeboat the therapist noted this saying 'she is so stubborn and has removed her dressing' – yes that was very much our employer.

Our mail deliveries at the Castle were always very late because of the distance. We all looked forward to the post and also what we called 'the bag'. This was any mail delivery from Clarence House specially delivered each day, whichever house we stayed in.

While at Sandringham one of our trips out that I enjoyed was a visit to Holkham Hall. I think it was there the spectacular lavender fields were. We were able to pick some lavender. When we got back to Clarence House we made and embroidered some little sachets to hold the lavender and placed them in any clothes drawers creating this lovely perfume. We also had pleasant afternoons at the beach or shopping in Kings Lynn. It made for very busy though enjoyable days as it was time for work on our return.

It was very different from my time working in Aberdeen when I was very much on my own most of the time.

Once or twice I had the pleasure of travelling on The Queen's Flight. These lovely red Andover planes felt really special and we were very well looked after. On one such flight there were a few girls and some of them were flirting with the crew. We were being served drinks and had turns listening on their headphones. On my turn I heard one of them say 'the girls are all boots and gin!'

It was after another flight the Air Commodore came to the Castle and sat chatting over tea in the staff hall, he was such a nice man. I was very sad some time later to hear Commodore Blunt had been killed when a plane he was travelling in crashed. I have never forgotten his name though I didn't know him well.

On another flight I felt very privileged to be one of a small group who would travel with The Queen. This was from RAF Benson to Wick. This flight was much more formal and we were spoiled and served a most delicious lunch of cold poached salmon.

All these years later it is so nice to think back on all these memories and keep them in my heart and mind forever though sometimes it can feel unreal. It was great being able to have enjoyed these adventures and taste a little bit of yet another different kind of life.

I was at the Castle for one of my birthdays when Peter Tappin our night sergeant handed me a small gift. It was one of those small cards with a tiny free sample of perfume called 'unforgettable' which he wrote on saying "that's what you are". Also enclosed were a few pounds with which he said 'buy yourself some'. Oh it was so emotional. I have that little card to this day. I liked Peter very much, we spent lots of time chatting together when he was on night duty. Sometime later I felt devastated to learn Peter had Leukaemia though he continued to work. I can also picture him standing outside the door at Birkhall with his arm on Robert's shoulder just the three of us. He looked up at the starry sky and said 'what's up there Rob?' at this time we did know of his illness. Peter did have four more years or so before giving up work. Writing this reminded me I had another birthday at the Castle way back when Maggie and Sandra were with us and Maggie gave me a tiny china trinket box with blue cornflowers and the words 'My wish for you is skies of blue' that too is a life time treasure. Many years later I bought one the same to give to Joan on her birthday on a special day I will be writing of later in my story.

Mrs Hards and I continued to enjoy our walk for half an hour each morning when on trips at Birkhall. We loved to walk around a circuit when we had the delightful pleasure to see the trees in their magnificent autumn colours. When at the Castle of Mey we either walked around the walled gardens or mostly to the sea to sit on The Queen's bench watching the seals. Very bracing and refreshing. She and I had many long chats together. The Queen liked to have the autumn leaves to decorate her morning breakfast tray.

I don't think Michael, our Chef, thought too much of the very cold frosty mornings and his antics over this used to make us laugh. Mind you the men slept in rooms above the garages and it could be really very cold. None of the house was heated, it made the beds all the more cosy.

Mrs Hards was able to go off with Norman in his red mini and meet some of his relatives in Aberdeen.

If at Birkhall when the Braemar Gathering was on we were able to go enjoying complimentary tickets to get in, this was always a great afternoon outing.

Chapter 14

The Boat Launch

With the grouse shooting season well underway and busy days preparing meals and packed lunches for the beaters, we were enjoying a spell of hot sunny days. After work today we were going on a staff outing with a very important mission. Bill, our chauffeur, had made quite a large and detailed model boat and today was to be its launch. We packed a small picnic and boarded our coach 'The Grey Lady' and there, on a specially made stand, the boat was placed on the floor by our feet looking resplendent. We were on our way to Loch Muick where the once much loved home of Queen Victoria was situated, sadly now unused it was set in the most glorious surroundings, it was not hard to imagine how special this place had been the sun shimmering on the water and the Mountains all round it looked magical. In just one instant it was gone, sinking in the deep loch, lost forever. It was very sad – though quite funny. I really did feel sorry for Bill, so much work and worse to travel back to Birkhall with the empty stand at our feet. I'll never forget the day of the boat launch!

At the Wednesday dances at Balmoral I found myself loving the fact that I had the most perfect dance partner. This was Jim, one of the gardeners, he was a great dancer, we danced so perfectly together and both of us loved this easy dancing. It was absolutely only the dancing, Jim's wife was always there. I did begin to worry as I could feel she didn't like the fact that Jim kept asking me to dance but his wife had bad legs and was unable to dance. I so loved dancing with him. I had no designs on him, or him on me, smooth and graceful dancing is just perfect and no harm was meant by this.

Back in London again it was nice to catch up with Helen who always worked on the opposite half of the trip to me. We always spent so much time together and Theresa, a housemaid, joined our get togethers. She used to give us all the London household news while we had been away. Some of the other non-travelling staff used to grumble because the staff coming back always said the food was so good that they felt they were missing out. It was hard for them to know it was because the milk was fresh from the churns, the bread and rolls not 'Mother's Pride' but delivered fresh from a local bakery each day, fresh and smelling delicious as well as the butcher so fresh it was easy to see how it was better. I'd heard that said a few times.

Mrs Hards and Norman were going to have a quiet wedding at her daughter's. They were given a flat at Kennington; she would now be Mrs Brown. She and Norman took me to see their home, it was a lovely big flat it must have felt so different from living at Clarence House for all those years. Now they travelled to work each day.

Sometimes there would be a conference at Lancaster House lasting late into the night then I would hear the cars being called for, one for each of the different ambassadors. It could be quite noisy, though I liked to lie in bed and listen to all the names called out as my room was right opposite Lancaster House.

Robert and I still worked the same weekends and we had some good laughs together. His friend Alan often came in to visit him. Alan had worked for a short time at Clarence House, he was young and very good looking, he used to flirt with me quite a lot. I did like Alan but did know that it was in my best interest to be careful; he didn't have any real intention of getting involved, because he had a strange nature and I felt unsure of his commitment to ladies.

There was a time over Christmas one year that I felt a sudden sad and lonely spell. I was on duty that year so couldn't go away. Some of the staff had gone to their homes and Helen was at Sandringham with the Queen. There were plenty of people left at Clarence House in reality, just not the younger set I was normally with. I had cooked the Christmas lunch and was free for the rest of the day. I decided to go to Epsom and see Meg and Celia. I got a train there okay but they were out. I hadn't arranged to visit. Back home I walked through St James's Park feeling quite alone and low. This was the first time I had a thought "is this how I'm going to spend the rest of my working years, perhaps I should change my job and my life if I'm never going to marry!" These were serious thoughts though I knew too that lack of confidence in myself would hold me back. I wasn't that keen on new things and guessed I would just leave it and stay where I was. I knew I had so enjoyed the life. I went back to the house. Bill Bridle, the policeman who let me in, asked if I'd been somewhere nice I lied and said I'd been at my sister Meg's. The next day I was fine again though had promised myself I would change my life at thirty and not be in service all my life.

If I'd been off duty I would have gone to Betty in Swindon; I had enjoyed visits to them a few times. I did really doubt if I'd have the courage to change this very comfortable life.

Once everyone was back and the house busy again I put these thoughts to the back of my mind, but they weren't forgotten.

Mrs Brown had now made her decision to retire and now after all these years as assistant cook I was being promoted to staff cook, which lifted my spirits. It was nice to be in charge of my own kitchen. I had a few changes of girls working with me; at one time I had two French girls Jocelyn and Annie. We had one or two fun times together. I remember one day someone had given me a joke jar of Colman's mustard and a snake type object popped out on opening the jar. I used the joke on Jocelyn and she screamed so loud even the Queen heard and asked had there been an accident in the kitchen! She scared me too!

At that time Barbara and Carol were in the Royal cooking side. Changes had been made and we all now worked in the Royal kitchen with new cookers added staff side. Michael made many changes.

Greta still came in to visit. We often went out together and we visited Pat. We all spent lots of time together. I used to take Pat's son Peter out sometimes and of course still visited Alison and John.

Greta said there was a dance at Knightsbridge Barracks. There was an invitation for nurses so Barbara, Carole and I joined her and went to the dance. That evening at the very last dance a tall young lad asked me to dance, his name was Tony.

We chatted for a time. He and his friends asked us if we'd like to see the horses so we went to the stables, I think they actually got told off for taking us there. Afterwards we walked home with the lads escorting us. As Tony and I walked along Constitution Hill he was telling me of how he had lost his brother Nigel in a car crash when he was only sixteen. It was very sad indeed, it seemed it had happened years before, I hadn't realised it was actually only months before in August and this was November. It must have still been very raw and painful for him and he really needed to talk about it. It was some months later before I registered that fact. As he left me at the gates Tony said he would like to take me out again and we arranged to do so. Barbara and Carole were going to meet John and Graham again too. Sometimes we went out in groups in those early days. In December I asked Tony if he would be my guest at our staff party. I put his name on the list, Robert was funny – he was convinced I'd made the name up as he had a less well known surname. He didn't believe I had a partner till he eventually met him.

The year I met Tony during the night of the 11th of December I woke with such a start at 4am and so out of the blue I thought of my Dad, I didn't understand my feelings, I was strange and unsettled. At 7am I had a phone call from Meg to say that our Dad had died at 4am. I was very shocked that I had wakened like that and felt that in spite of all the years we'd lived apart, neither seeing nor hearing much of each other, to me it shows there was a very real bond of something binding us together in our very being, the feeling was very unreal.

Meg, Betty and I all made plans to travel to Scotland for our Dads funeral. Like Geordie, Meg had made quite a few trips home to our Mum and Dad's over the years and Celia too had met her grandparents.

I had been going to meet Tony that night so I left a letter for him at the police lodge.

All my family were there for Dad's funeral, it was a very strange feeling to have all of us sit around a big table being served homemade soup by Mary and Bunty, each quiet with our own thoughts and emotions. I'll remember it always, the day was unreal, with a thousand emotions for all of us I should think. I can't imagine what our mother's feelings were having all of her children around her.

In the church I could hear people talking behind us trying to decide who each of us were. I'm sure there were plenty of words and thoughts being whispered and not all favourable to us. It had been a very strange day. Betty and I travelled back to London on the train together so got the chance to have a good chat about it all.

Tony became a more regular visitor to me and gradually got to know all my friends. I made a point of telling him of my family life. I knew very well that this made no difference to him, if you care for someone it should be just about the person you got to know and had feelings for, that, I feel, is the right way for a relationship.

Sometimes Tony and I visited Greta and Lucky at his flat. We had some very enjoyable evenings together there was always so much going on. One of our police lodge team, I think his name was Tony, had a friend who had some involvement in a clothes business and came in with some lovely dresses for us to look through and buy. I think he, along with John, a footman, and Helen too came to a party at Lucky's flat.

John had been with us a few years, he came from the Orkney Islands. I liked John, he and Terry were good friends... mostly! John had met Janet, a very nice girl, and they eventually became engaged. One day in the grounds of Clarence House, while he was out walking the dogs, he saw and was able to catch a parakeet that had flown into the garden. After trying hard to find out the ownership of the bird with no success he chose to keep it and called it Clarence, this was a great novelty to everyone. Soon John and Janet were going to be married and Clarence would be their pet.

Tony and I had an invitation to John and Janet's wedding in Reading where they were to live, for John was leaving Clarence House. Janet looked lovely and carried white lilies for her bouquet. It was nice that day to see some old faces as one former staff member, Carol, was there with her husband and children. She had gone on to work for Lady Fermoy as cook and Barry as her chauffeur and handyman.

Tony had got to know Alison and John, I think he even babysat for them one night. I can't think of when I gave up the agency babysitting, perhaps when I was too busy going out with Tony. I had loved it meeting the children and seeing all the lovely houses. Again, I can't think why I got talked into a one afternoon a week cleaning job at the flat of Mr and Mrs Buchanan, but extra money was always useful. Mr Buchanan was the Lord Chamberlain and had a flat in Ambassadors Court so it was nice and near. I also did a spring clean in one of the Queen's gentlemen's flats, that of Sir Martin Gilliat, again in Ambassadors Court, that was just a favour and for one week. I can't think how I got myself into these extras!

Pat and I continued to be good friends and to spend time together. When it was Peter's third birthday we had a little party in my room for him, I spent a lot of time with Peter.

These days my family were all settled in their chosen lives. Some years ago John chose to have a very quiet wedding, his new wife Margaret is so lovely, but I haven't lived near enough to be able to spend a lot of time with them. I know she loves being part of the Young family and we love having her in our lives. I feel so lucky to be able to say I really like all of both my sisters in law and brothers in law: Jackie, Margaret, Brian, Eric and Willie, all nice and welcome additions to our family.

I'm very proud of the fact that none of my family were ever out of work, none were ever in any trouble, all going on to have made good responsible lives for themselves and their families. I think that is a very good record for such a large family, John has been in the same job for all of his working life.

When in Aberdeen to visit Mary and Willie I was delighted to hear that Geordie too was going to be married to Doris. I had not met Doris but as I was going to be in Aberdeen at the time of their wedding I made sure I was there to see them going in to be married. Now there was only Bunty, Meg and I who were single.

Chapter 15

The Life Guards

Tony was in the mounted division of the regiment to exercise the horses, they would ride through the streets in the very early morning, part of practise for ceremonial duties. They had some good laughs during this time. This day Tony was on Hector, a large drum horse, and riding through the streets to Knightsbridge he showed his character it seemed and felt a poor horse can get very tired and on seeing a stationary bus Hector placed his big foot on the bus causing Tony great amusement when the Indian bus conductor said 'horse, horse get off my bus' poor Hector had to walk! Tony said it was very, very funny. The horses were so well trained they knew the way themselves and if the soldier was particularly tired after a night out, practically asleep while riding, the horse knowing the route led them round. This of course was not permitted but did happen with the antics of these young soldiers.

This time Tony was my guest for the Windsor Castle Ball, always a very enjoyable night out. Terry also came with us this time, this wasn't the greatest idea as sometimes he did drink too much, his nerves were quite bad and he did get himself into trouble and would be 'egged on' by Billy and Reg who liked to drag him down. As I said earlier I did look out for Terry as much as I could.

When the warmer weather came Tony and I, along with Carol and Graham, packed a picnic to have on a day out at the Tower of London, we had a great day.

On our return home Tony's cream coloured trousers were stained with beetroot juice from the salad – not a good look! Though he was very good about the fact that I had packed beetroot, I tease him now saying 'you loved me then and never moaned as you would now!' We have joked over that on occasion.

As we were soon to go to Scotland Tony asked me if I would marry him. I was taken by surprise and felt I couldn't answer right then so asked him to wait until after the Scotland trip and I would give him my answer. I was really scared to commit and perhaps get it wrong, indecisive, yes, that was me true to my Libra star sign.

I was talking to Mary Kenny, a housemaid, I liked Mary – she was sensible, I mentioned Tony to her and she said 'that's a young man with a very honest face he'll never let you down,' I liked that, it helped but I was still scared to commit.

We were back in Scotland, as always it was nice to see everyone again and settle into a routine. I was always the first one in the kitchen each morning, I liked to get organised and to get my first choice of the ovens, a crafty move. Jim, a detective, used to come in for a cup of tea, he was a fellow Scot and nice to chat with.

Terry didn't seem to be too well and the doctor had to be called in, his pain was very severe, he had pleurisy and he was to go into hospital in Aberdeen. At least we knew he would be well looked after.

Someone came to me one day saying there is a young lad working at Balmoral who says he knows you. I was very surprised to learn that this was Andrew Laing who was a student working at Balmoral, it was nice to see this now grown up young man who I had last seen when he was twelve. I sat and chatted to him and yet I didn't have the courage to ask him about his sister Alison who had throat cancer. He seemed a very nice young lad and I was pleased to see him at the dances that season and to know his parents were well.

Jim, the gardener, was still there and again we enjoyed the dances, he was a great dancer and we enjoyed partnering each other.

It was while we were at the Castle of Mey that I wrote to Tony saying I would be happy for us to become engaged when I got back.

Terry was still in hospital so I made the effort to travel into Aberdeen to visit him. He was so pleased to see me and was making a good recovery.

I had been able to visit all my friends while on holiday before our half at Birkhall.

Mrs Davidson was pleased when I told her Tony and I were to become engaged and said to invite him to Scotland for a holiday.

Once we were settled back in London, Tony and I chose to make the first of November our engagement date, this was Tony's twenty first birthday. I had been to Ramsgate to meet his Mum and Dad. It did concern me they looked so young as I was eight years older than Tony, were we right for each other, I really did have all these thoughts. It was nice to meet his sister Theresa, her boyfriend Geoff, and his Grandmother. Everyone was very nice and made me feel very welcome when they knew of our engagement plans. Sheila and Les, his parents, hired a hall and planned a party for us, it was a most enjoyable evening, so many of my friends joined us, Alison and John, Greta and Lucky, Helen, I think Pat and John, I'm sure Meg came as well. Quite a few of us stayed overnight and Tony's Mum and Dad's house was very crowded, I met a lot of Tony's relatives that night.

At Clarence House everyone seemed very surprised at our engagement for some reason a few of them thought I'd never marry. They all liked my ring, I remember Miss Jones our housekeeper saying 'I never knew you had such beautiful hands Alice!' It had been fun choosing the ring – poor Tony – I walked him all round Oxford Street, Regent Street and everywhere then back to the very first shop we'd been in and chose a ring with a very lovely diamond cluster. I couldn't wait to show everyone though I had to leave it in the shop to be taken in and then, of course, kept till the 1st of November.

Now we really were a couple and would soon start to make plans for our future. Greta and Lucky invited us for a celebration dinner at Gloucester Terrace, a most enjoyable evening.

When the staff were lined up in the garden at the Queen's request to see a major procession pass down The Mall I remember Mr Taylor, our steward, say to me 'I saw your young man tip his sword in salute to us,' of course he could never do that. It was very hard to pick anyone out as they all looked so resplendent and exactly the same in their red tunic and brass breast plates, a wonderful sight. Those days were very special moments in time for us. Tony was fortunate to have been on many important functions, The Lord Mayors Show, Princess Anne's wedding, plenty Trooping of the Colours, The Garter Service at Windsor, and no doubt some I haven't thought of. He had been on The Musical Ride, at Earls Courts Royal Tournament, I think it was six years he was in The Mounted Regiment, then he was posted to Windsor to join the armored side of The Life Guards as was the custom. He had loved his time in London and of course he was stationed in Windsor now so he had to travel to London to see me. I did remind him we would have to save money now for our wedding as we were going to pay for all of it ourselves.

At Christmas Tony and I stayed at Betty and Brian's in Swindon. Tony and Brian got on so well together, I was pleased at that, we really enjoyed any times we stayed with them.

I now had to get used to the fact that Tony would sometimes have to go away on exercise, this was all new to me, though no problem while at Clarence House with all my friends.

This did give me time to think of our wedding planning. My first thought was to choose October, my birthday month. Greta said a spring wedding would be nice so April the 9th was chosen to be our special day. This was to be in 1977.

For my choice of bridesmaids I asked Helen and made a visit to Meg's to ask Celia. She was very thrilled, Celia would be almost fourteen then.

Thinking that the next trips to Birkhall and Castle of Mey would be my last I felt quite sad really but had lots to think about. Terry was having a lot of work related problems through too much drinking, this was creating a crisis point and he was devastated that they planned to retire him through ill health. This was very hard after twenty three years of service and led to a complete breakdown for Terry. I don't think it helped him being put into a psychiatric hospital. Tony and I visited him in there, he was not in a good place in his mind, I felt very concerned for him. I continued to visit him and Captain Aird said 'thank you' to me for looking out for Terry. He was my friend and I cared for him. His mind rested, but far from well, they found a post for him in another household thinking it would be much less stressful, this was to work for Lady Chulmley. Terry was very unhappy and hated it. Something more suited to him was found, working for Mr Jewel, a gentleman, and he began to recover, though he was never happy at having to leave Clarence House. It had been his life and I knew so well of his complete loyalty to the Queen, he thought the world of her, much more so than Billy and Reg whose real only concern was the lifestyle they had created and loved. I know, I saw it all first hand over my fourteen years, I was really very wise to their ways.

Over the next weeks Helen and I found ourselves on less friendly terms, very silly I know now as really it was over our different opinions about Terry having to leave Clarence House, we each had out own views. Helen went off to work at Sandingham over the festive season. I had thoughts that I had made a mistake over my choice of bridesmaids as I had known and been friends with Greta for much longer.

On her return I went down to talk this over with Helen, I assured her I much valued our friendship and would always think that way, she would help in any way she could.

I felt very sad to know if I had only asked Greta in the first place I would not have hurt Helen, I was not proud of myself as I loved Helen then as I do now, I did have my reason for this as Helen and I were similar in size and along with my niece Celia who was nearly fourteen we would all be the same in photos.

Tony was going to Edinburgh on exercise so I said if you get some free time go and introduce yourself to my sister Chris, Eric and Marianne and Lee, they lived in Rosyth. Tony did this and took some chocolate buttons for the children. The day was very hot reminding me to say to him 'you say the weather is never nice in Scotland!' The buttons were all melted and they had to eat them with a spoon! Chris said in a letter 'he will make a nice brother in law.'

Our wedding plans were underway; we had booked the church and the Amatola Hotel in Aberdeen for our reception.

Now I was ready for my last spell at Birkhall and Castle of Mey, quite a sad thought. This at least gave me the chance to say goodbye to everyone.

When on holiday Tony was going to join me to meet Mr and Mrs Davidson, we were going to stay a week with them. I felt very touched at how they put themselves so outside their usual ways to make a good impression for Tony and make him feel welcome. They had booked a table at a local lounge bar where there was a group playing, it was really nice of them. Mr Davidson's health wasn't very good at this time. We enjoyed our week, with me showing Tony round the area and having walks by the River Don. It was a nice holiday.

On our return to London Tony was asked to be best man for his friend Paul. This was to be in Sheffield. When we travelled there Paul's Mum and Dad were so welcoming, they were Polish, we were amazed at how much they expected us to eat, their food was wonderful. The wedding day was perfect and we so much enjoyed the hospitality of the special couple.

Alison and John were soon going back to Germany, as always, I would miss having them to visit.

There was a lot to do as I had planned to make my wedding dress and to make our wedding cake a bit nearer the time and to plan to meet with Meg and Celia along with Greta to choose bridesmaids' dresses. It was a really nice fun shopping spree choosing dresses, Celia and Greta felt happy, the choice was apricot coloured flared dresses with tiny flowers, so lovely! I was delighted. It was while they were trying various dresses that Meg said to me 'what would you think if I said I wanted to marry someone from Ghana?' I replied 'if it's right for you Meg it is your choice, I'll be happy for you.' Meg said "Paul is meeting Celia and I later if you would like to come and meet him" and that is what I did.

There was a lot to do in the next months choosing our menu for the reception. Tony was at home in Ramsgate when I phoned him to discuss this before getting in touch with the hotel to confirm our choice. I organised the wording on our invitations a bit different as this wasn't a Mother and Father's invitation. Tony and I completely covered our own wedding costs, Mr Davidson was happy to walk me down the aisle. It was all getting much nearer and an exciting and busy time.

Miss Jones was, as always, very kind she asked me if she could get me any 'bottom drawer' items at cost prices, this was a big saving getting all our towels and bedding. I also bought two trunks for packing – a very useful buy. I was offered a lovely hand woven rug from an embassy, it was large and beautiful.

I made our three cake tiers in the kitchen at Clarence House and sent them to be iced at Renshaws as we did over the years with our Christmas cakes, this was perfect as they would have them delivered to the hotel in Aberdeen. I was amazed at how little they charged me to have this done and very delighted. They most certainly gave me a very special rate.

It was all coming together and we were very lucky indeed to receive so many wonderful wedding gifts, including a dinner service of my choice from a collection from staff and household along with so many individual gifts. We felt very fortunate, from the Queen I was to be presented with a mahogany tea trolley – the very last one of this type to be made by Mr Keen, a furniture maker. Miss Jones told me it was all very exciting.

It was hard for me to believe how little time I had left at Clarence House, I had very strange feelings thinking of entering a whole new life.

Miss Jones wanted me to choose a tea set as a personal gift from her. She had been so kind to me, having given me all sorts of items since my engagement, to this day we still make great use of a tray she just handed me one night. I was on supper duty and she said 'would you like this Alice?' It so often makes me think of her kindness.

My last day finally came, Tony's friend Graham had come with a van one evening the week before and collected my trunks and our gifts and taken them to Windsor where our new home would be.

That last day I had to be ready to be presented to the Queen in the drawing room. We had received the trolley and she gave me a white gold brooch as a personal gift. As she chatted to me for a few minutes I said how much I'd miss Birkhall she said 'you can still have the walks up there you enjoyed' so that was nice. Then, as was the custom, I left money behind the canteen bar to buy drinks for everyone. After my farewells I travelled on an all night sleeper train to Aberdeen as I had to reside there for three weeks to have our banns called out in church. It was a strange feeling all these complete changes taking place once more to alter my life forever, and believe me I most certainly felt the emotion of it all.

'Big sigh' right Alice, here comes the rest of my life whatever it holds!

When back home I had lots of things to check up on at the florist and the photographer, making my hair appointment, arranging the cars, so it kept me busy.

Mr and Mrs Davidson wanted me to choose a wedding gift, I think they were rather surprised at my choice of crystal decanter and glasses, they really favoured more practical, everyday using gifts. She understood when I said I intended one day to have a crystal cabinet as I had collected many crystal items from the Queen as Christmas gifts over the years. Mrs Davidson and I picked the set I have been delighted to enjoy over all these years.

The next couple of weeks were busy with lots of visits from friends coming to bring us gifts.

I was delighted to see my friend Tom and Mary his wife on the Sunday though very shocked to know Tom was suffering from multiple sclerosis at an advanced stage though he assured me he would still be at my wedding, his illness did make me sad as I hadn't realised. Tom was delighted to know of my wedding and to be invited. It would have been unthinkable for me not to have him there.

The day or so before I went to Aberdeen to meet Sheila and Les who had travelled by coach and Tony and his best man Graham who travelled on the overnight train, I had booked a table at a nearby hotel for us all to enjoy breakfast.

I was going to stay in Aberdeen with Mary and Willie as I was going to leave from her house as a bride.

We were a bit sad Tony's sister Theresa was going to miss the wedding as she was awaiting the birth of her first baby and we were delighted to get the news that Russell was born four days before our wedding and all was well though Sheila felt a bit upset at not being there for her daughter having a baby.

Everything was ready.

Tony had some friends arriving from London and they were going to enjoy a stag night together while Sheila was going to join me at Mary's for the evening. There were a few other people there with me to enjoy my last night as a single girl.

Chapter 16

Our Wedding Day

I woke up early in the morning of this day it was the ninth of April 1977. I had an appointment at the hairdresser and Greta did too, Celia and Mr Davidson were going to arrive later. There was a snow shower but no snow on the ground, everything seemed to be going as planned, the waiting did make me feel nervous, and at last it was time. Everyone else had gone and my bridesmaids' car had just driven off with Greta and Celia both looking very beautiful. Mr Davidson and I were both nervous as we set off in our lovely hired car for the church. I was glad it was dry for all the photos that were taken before Mr Davidson walked me down the aisle. It was so lovely to see so many of my special relatives and friends there. We were Mr and Mrs Tony Taft, wow, can this be real?

I was much more relaxed as we made our way to the reception now escorted by my new husband. We waited in the foyer to say 'hello' to our guests. I had a very big surprise to see someone I knew who simply came to the hotel to enjoy lunch as an hotel guest along with her mother, Mrs Anderson, telling me they were celebrating that Stella had just passed her Doctorate. We hugged congratulating each other before they left for their lunch.

The reception was truly delightful even though some important friends couldn't join us. This included Alison, John and their boys, Pat and John and Mrs Brown and Norman who had her daughter's special celebration. We heard from them all and Pat's Mum and her younger sister were outside the church with a horseshoe to present to me. I was sorry to know later that Sandy's daughter Sandra had also been there and I hadn't seen her, I did wish she had come forward.

Terry and his friends and a group of Tony's friends joined us as well as John and Janet. It was wonderful to have Joan,

Max, Emma, my god-daughter, and brother Andrew and many others. Of course it was a long way for people to come. We had eighty guests. This day was Joan's birthday so I had planned for Tony to wish her happy birthday at the end of his speech. She was a bit stunned having to come forward to accept the little china dish with the words 'my wish for you is skies of blue' the same as Maggie had given me years before, that I had so loved.

It had been a perfect day, with some friends saying that it was the best wedding they had ever been to, so that was nice. So many nice memories of the day, such as Chris's eighteen month old son feeling hungry while we waited to be seated and Miss Urquhart an invited guest (as she was now a friend who had played a major part in our childhood) little Lee decided to have a roll, she jokingly said 'I hope that's not mine,' precious moments! Lee was so beautiful with his blond curly hair and wearing his kilt.

Tony and I stayed at the hotel that night. We planned to stay a week in Aberdeen before travelling to Windsor. After another night in a hotel we went to Chris and Eric's, of course Tony and Eric chose to go to the pub – Chris saying 'don't you stay out late keeping Tony from his honeymoon,' that was quite funny. As they came home at a reasonable time and it was Chris and I who stayed up till after 3.30am chatting!

Tony and I had to buy some tea chests to have our gifts from Scotland packed and transported. By this time our funds were very low but we made it. When eventually on the train journey from London to Windsor I must have looked thoughtful as Tony looked at me and said 'don't worry, I will look after you my love.' That was nice; here we were at the start of our life together.

It was Friday when we arrived in Windsor. As it was late in the day we were too late to get the keys for our first married quarter. Tony had arranged for us to spend the weekend with his friends Bev and Maurice, they were very nice and welcoming. On the Saturday they took us to the nearby Slough shopping centre. I felt a bit out of sorts as I was eager to set up our own home. It was nice to have met Bev and Maurice I didn't know them before now, at least I had a new friend in Windsor.

Our first house was an older property; there was lots to do to make it our own. There was a lovely big garden and a small shop just around the corner. Graham came to deliver my trunks which he had collected from Clarence House. This was all very new for me to get used to, I really did miss all my friends and having lots of people around.

Gradually we settled in to this new routine, this was still all so strange, I no longer could walk over to Pat's at Marlborough House or sit and chat with Helen. I really did need to find some work as I felt quite lonely.

John Spence came to visit as he and Janet lived in Reading. When he left he found some factory work and said why didn't I apply to work there as there was a special bus from Windsor.

I didn't really like the idea as I wanted to be cooking, though as John said 'the money was very good' and I really needed to work and keep busy as Tony was soon to be on a four month tour in the very troubled Northern Ireland.

I did get the job, which was shift work from 6am till 2pm one week then 2pm till 10pm next. I really didn't like the late shift. It was in a car bearings factory, I really didn't like the work either, but it wouldn't be forever and I did make some new friends and became more settled. Bev and I met up sometimes and an elderly couple who travelled on the coach with me became real friends. They lived near to us, Mac was Scottish, and he took a real liking to me, insisting I visit. He and his wife Connie were both so lovely and took me to their hearts. When Tony did go to Ireland they really looked out for me. I enjoyed the fact I could save money, I'd never had such big wages, I decided I'd buy Tony a new music centre as he loved music so much. During his time away when I had a day off I went to London to visit everyone. I had been back once already to deliver cake boxes for everyone and to show our wedding album, it was really nice to see everyone and Robert promised he would come for a visit.

Some days later I thought it was very nice to receive letters from some of the household gentlemen and Lady Jean Rankin and Lady Fermoy as well as Mrs Mullholland, The Queen's lady in waiting, thanking me for the cake, I hadn't expected that, all nice keepsakes.

It sounded very funny to me to be allocated a 'Regimental Father' while our men were on tours such as this, someone to turn to in the event we would need it, we did have news of bombings that caused us concern. Mostly the wives just got together at these times, of course I wrote lots of letters to Tony they all so looked forward to their mail each day.

Eventually the tour ended and Tony was back home, they still had short exercises away for a few days.

Tony's Mum and Dad sometimes came for a weekend and Theresa, Geoff and baby Russell, making us think of having a baby.

Greta came for a weekend now and then. We sometimes went for long walks in Windsor Great Park, I felt much more settled and I liked Windsor.

I had met some of Tony's friends and had some small house parties and there were plenty of functions to attend at the Barracks especially the summer ball, I loved that. Bev and Maurice were with us that night and Bev was eager to find out if I'd confirmed that I was having my first baby and 'yes' I was and Tony and I were delighted at the prospect of being parents.

I continued working as long as possible as Tony was away on exercise a few times, Connie and Mac always looked out for me, I liked them very much.

I did suffer sickness for most of the first seven months, in spite of that I loved being pregnant, I worked till Christmas – friends telling me I would need to go back for only two weeks after to get extra money but I choose not to, shift work wasn't that comfortable at this stage and my baby was due on the 23rd of February. I was thirty two years old and considered an older mother for my first baby. It was nice to have those few weeks to relax before the event.

My due date came and went, four days later I was admitted to Heatherwood Hospital in Royal Ascot. There was a major ambulance dispute at the time. Heatherwood had made plans for me to go to another hospital for a scan and a car had to be organised to take me, this never happened as that night at 9pm it all started to happen and I was taken to the delivery ward where I had a very long night ahead of me. I wanted them to call Tony and was told 'not yet' there's plenty of time. It was 4am when they called the Barracks to call Tony to the hospital, I was so excited and eager for him to get there, it took ages. I later heard of the trouble they had to wake him up having to throw stones at the windows. Eventually he awoke and was driven to Heatherwood, I had been looking at the sleety rain at the windows above my head and the nurse checking on me every few minutes, this scene I remember always. I was pleased when Tony arrived, a few hours later he was starving and went for some breakfast and came back pacing the corridor. The lady in the next delivery room later told me she would remember Tony's face, always so concerned as he kept passing her room. It felt a very long time before a Doctor came in to assess the situation and the nurses told him that I had been very good and tolerant. The decision was made I needed a last second emergency caesarean section. Our new son was finally delivered at 1.25pm. I did hear it said 'it's a boy', but was very much out of it. Some hours later I sort of saw Tony telling me we have a little boy, I was trying to answer 'yes I know' I was just so very tired I perhaps only thought I'd said it.

Tony had been able to hold and feed our baby whilst he was in the special care unit. I was still very dazed the next morning when two nurses were getting me up to fix my bed, what my confused thoughts were I don't know but remember saying on hearing them talking 'no I'm not going there again!'

Later that morning I had recovered enough to ask a staff nurse 'how is my baby' I didn't feel her compassion as she stood there and said 'he's in special care' giving me no real clue if all was well. She did leave me distressed, only relaxing a couple of hours later when our son was placed in his cot next to my bed, he was a very beautiful, fairly big baby as was just under 8lbs. We named him Christopher Nigel Taft, middle name in memory of Tony's late brother, his Mum Sheila was very delighted at that and any future cards were always written to our dear Christopher Nigel. We had lots of flowers, gifts and cards and a visit from Pat, John and I think Helen. I was ten days in hospital after the birth.

A friend of Tony's came to drive us home, there was a layer of snow on the ground this February, no, March, morning as

Christopher was born on the 28th of February the last day of the month.

I felt so strange on that journey, I was holding our new son and had the strange feeling I was holding him at arm's length yet I wasn't. When indoors that unreal feeling continued, I asked Tony what shall I do with him? It is a very emotional time that's for sure! His little basket had been made all warm and cosy for him and I gradually felt real again, those emotions were very strong for me, I know for sure the real emotional turmoil of having a first baby. Tony was actually meant to be away on exercise in Denmark, I think while I was in hospital when the Doctor was in my room I had asked him to write to the Barracks and ask for Tony to be excused from the exercise as after the operation I felt concerned to be on my own with a new baby. The Doctor was lovely, though that, I felt, disagreeable staff nurse was with him and tried to butt in saying 'no you must go to your family Doctor for that.' The Doctor or surgeon as he was said 'no it's fine I can do that she does need to feel secure.'

Tony's Mum and Dad came to see their new Grandson. On Sunday they chose to go out for a before lunch drink of course I couldn't join them and admit to feeling a thought of oh this is how it will be from now on; it was all very new being a mummy.

I think it was before I had Christopher that Robert did come and stay for a few days with me while Tony was away. It was lovely to see him and chat over news of everyone, he enjoyed the visit very much saying he was made to feel very welcome. It was almost the same time as I had a visit from Joan and her children Emma and Andrew. Joan only just missed seeing Robert and was sorry to have done so. I was sad to know Joan and Max parted and were going to divorce. Joan felt happier to have made her decision. It was lovely to have them visit.

It was so special when Christopher gave me that first real smile, at that moment I felt a change in me and knew I loved being a Mummy, not like the first weeks of strange emotions, now we really were a family and I loved being a wife and mother.

Sandra, my friend in Canada, had written telling me she was having her first baby. This was in the days when I was in hospital before I gave birth so that was great news and I was able to write Sandra a very long and detailed letter of my thoughts and feelings over the past weeks. She was so pleased saying how much the letter had helped her as she too had all the strange emotions as she also had a caesarean birth. It gave me a big lift to feel I had helped. In our letters, we have always supported each other, they have been important to us both.

It was very nice news that Tony and I were going to have Mr and Mrs Davidson come and stay a few days with us, their son Robbie and wife Marian had taken them on the long drive from Scotland. This was a big trip for them as I don't think they had ever been out of Scotland.

Robbie and Marian were going on to stay with friends.

We had an enjoyable few days, took them to London and let them see all the sights, they enjoyed the holiday and to see Christopher who was about two months old.

Plans were being made for the regiment to move to Germany, this was going to be another big change for us. It was going to be early in the next year so Christopher would be around one year old.

We made plans for Christopher to be christened. I cut my wedding dress to make a christening gown and made a buffet for after; we invited quite a few friends. Meg, Paul and Celia were going to come and Betty, Brian and Gordon, we had last got together in the December after our wedding as Meg and Paul married that same year as we did. Betty, Brian, Tony and I travelled to Epsom for their special day, our Auntie Mary came from Scotland to be there, she was our Dad's sister and loved to be involved in the family. Meg looked lovely and we all enjoyed a party at their new house afterwards. I thought it was a lovely house and I liked the name 'Arranleith' it sounded Scottish.

Alan and Geoff, who both worked at Clarence House, came for the christening, Geoff driving me back home after in his smart sports car so that I could be first and set the food out. It was a great party, Connie and Mac came, Alison and John and their four boys, Tony's Mum and Dad and Nan and some of Tony's friends. It was a very special day that I loved and having both Meg and Betty there was extra special.

As we were in Windsor we were nearer to Betty and Brian to be able to visit them and were pleased to be able to invite them to our summer ball at the Barracks. I knew Betty would enjoy this special event.

Meg and Paul let us know they were going to have a baby as we were starting to pack ready to move to Germany. Tony and I planned to go to Ramsgate to visit his Mum, Dad, Theresa, Geoff and son Russell and held a party at their house inviting some of their relatives. By this time I knew I was having another baby, I remember telling Greta when she phoned that night. This was the first I'd mentioned it, everyone was very pleased, Theresa my sister in law was also having her second baby – so it was babies all round.

It was a busy time getting all our home packed up for our move, exciting too at the thought of yet another different life, I had no idea how it would all be.

There was the experience of our army house handover to come over the years, I was to learn the major work this created.

When the day came Christopher and I went to have breakfast with Connie and Mac while Tony completed our handover, I knew I would miss Connie's friendship, I promised we'd keep in touch.

All our travelling was sorted out for us, our flight from Luton to Gutersloh, then a coach to Detmold near Paderborn, it was all very exciting, or at least I thought so till I heard the unsavoury language of a mother to her children and thought I hope she won't be my next door neighbour.

On arrival we were served refreshments while names of families were sorted out for coaches. It seemed most people had gone then we were last and there was a car to take us to our estate. It seemed to me a long drive, were we miles from anyone? I had no idea our estate was Amposteich, I liked the name. It was late and too dark to see much of our surroundings.

We were very tired as we were let into our flat but wow! It was so big I loved the big window and balcony, it felt very grand. There was a starter food pack with eggs, bacon, milk, bread, tea and coffee.

So, left only with beds to sort out, we had no boxes arrived as yet, with no radio it was just tea, relax, settle Christopher, get the feel of the place and after an exhausting day it was bedtime.

Chapter 17

Amposteich

The next morning I was very impressed at the view from our big window in the flat. There was a frosty mist enveloping the scene, it was breath-taking to see all the frost covered pine trees and red squirrels darting up them. We were on the second floor and right at the edge of the wood. Christopher loved seeing the squirrels, in Windsor it was the planes especially Concorde he loved to see. I still loved letter writing it would be a joy to describe this scene.

Tony took the bus to the Naafi to stock up the cupboards and returned with a television for us, there were very few English programmes, at least we could get the news.

Our boxes arrived and much of the day was spent unpacking.

Life was going to be very different here from Windsor. There was a bus each day to the medical centre in the barracks, and on to the Naafi, as I was four months pregnant I had to register soon.

This was February 1980, six days before Christopher's first birthday.

The estate was set out in rows of four front doors to each block, from the kitchen we overlooked a grassed area with a play area including a sandpit and two more rows of flats in front of ours. Our washing lines were just at the edge of the wood, there I liked to hear a woodpecker tapping at the tree.

It was nice getting to know some of the other families, Tony of course knew most of the men and introduced me as we met. None of the people I had got to know in Windsor were on our estate so I knew no one, though having children always breaks the ice.

This was how I came to know Chris; as we stood waiting for the Naafi bus she had her son, Tony, who was the same age as

Christopher and like me was having her second baby. We chatted together and I invited Chris to come over for coffee later in the day. Chris was to become another lifetime friend, we were so opposite in many ways and yet we would share many adventures together over the next four years. Chris and John lived in the same row as we did and Tony and Christopher played well together.

Connie, my friend in Windsor, soon wrote back saying how much she loved my letter describing our new home and said she and Mac could picture the whole scene as it was so well described.

We had a little shop nearby, the lady, who only spoke German, was very kind and helpful. I was quite nervous shopping there at first it felt very strange to get used to their way of greeting and saying as they do.

Our men were so often away on exercise, especially on that first year, so we spent much of our time together going out for walks with our children.

Our days filled with check-up appointments creating some adventure too like the time another wife, Sue, and I had travelled all the way to Rinteln, a couple of hours away, to be told this was the wrong date for us! They did see us and we had our scan and had to await an ambulance going back to Detmold to get us home.

I was eager to get home that day as Tony and I had bought some new carpet and furniture, and it was all being delivered that day when Tony was at home. I had to find my own way back from the medical centre so went to my friend Jean who drove me home to what felt like a different house that Tony had put all in order, just finishing off even if I later found that my Beswick horse had sustained an injured leg where Christopher had held it by the leg and it snapped. Superglue is magic and holds it to this day!

Chris had to be taken to the Krankenhaus to have her baby as she wouldn't have made it to Rinteln, their baby daughter was to be called Natalie.

On our estate there was quite a few parties either in the flats or often in the cellars decked out with camouflage netting, we had some great times at these events, or just get togethers in our flats. Tony's Mum and Dad, Sheila and Les to me, loved to come over for a holiday from Ramsgate and enjoyed these get togethers. Jane and Kevin our friends came for the evening, Jane and I both with big bumps, Jane having her first baby. We had some great laughs playing charades, they were happy times. Of course Chris and John were always in our lives, we spent so much time together.

One day I went on the bus to go to the medical centre as Christopher wasn't very well, he did get some medicine. We weren't long indoors before two of my neighbours came in with a new coffee table I had ordered to complete our new look home. Christopher was causing me concerns, especially when he went into a convulsion frightening me to bits. Thankfully Barbara, who was a mother of four, knew how to handle this, cooling him down and Marlesse drove us to the medical centre – who decided he should go to Rintein B.M.H. We travelled by ambulance. This was only ten days before I was booked in to have my baby. Tony was away on exercise at the time. After assessment Christopher was admitted just to keep an eye on him. I had a bed in a room where I could look through to his ward, I got no rest at all and was very uncomfortable with my advanced pregnancy. The nurses noting this called me through to their office in the middle of the night to sit and have tea with them. I had asked for Tony to be called and got distressed at thinking they hadn't called him the next day. He did arrive later in the day driven by Grant our next door neighbour and was pleased that we were allowed home with them.

Christopher was very young and I was trying to get him to understand Mummy was going to be going to hospital to bring home our new baby. Tony's Mum and Dad were going to come over and look after him; I hated the thought of leaving him.

July 31st was my day to go in and soon after being given the ghastly enema and left in a really large bathroom a scene that seemed could only be seen in a comedy farce took place. This wasp chose to buzz around my face as I went to sit on the toilet and I ended running round the bathroom chased by the wasp – not a pretty sight at nine months pregnant. It would not go away, if seen by anyone it would have seemed very funny. When I finally escaped I told Tony, him knowing I wasn't very brave with wasps as it was.

The next morning given toast that was almost burnt, I was taken to the labour ward to be induced, the toast had given me serious heartburn, the nurse said she would give me something to help. The next six hours I was in there having contractions. Tony was with me and believe this or not, he too was suffering the pains! I even said 'are you sure you weren't out drinking last night', he assured me 'no', he felt very ill. I wanted the window open, this very hot August day, he wanted it closed. I said to the nurse 'how much longer will this take', she said 'I'll get my crystal ball out for you in a minute!' I had a doctor on standby in case I needed another 'C' section, I was so pleased this wasn't needed and elated to be now in the delivery room where at one twenty five our second son was born. This time being able to hold him straight away was very special, I loved the fact both our boys were born at just exactly the same time of the day one on the first day of the month and one on the last day of the month.

We named our baby Stuart William Taft; he weighed a healthy seven pounds. William was chosen after my brother.

Tony was still feeling really ill and told me later that he had a sleep on the grass in the shade of a tree, this day was very hot. I was on my own when they came back with a form that had to be signed to declare he had been born in a British Military Hospital so wouldn't have to go into the German army, it sounded funny with him just born. The next day I wanted to go and have a bath though I was supposed to have waited for help in case I felt faint. I ran the bath taps fully and when they wouldn't turn off I was in a panic, it was nearly full, I ran into the corridor, the first person I saw was a young Doctor in his white coat, poor man I grabbed him by the sleeve, pulling him in to turn the taps off. I had visions of flooding the hospital corridor, the poor man was stunned. I later realised it was very funny and that was my second comedy moment.

I had to be in there two weeks as Stuart was jaundiced and under a special light, I felt quite proud when on the Doctors round they used me as an example to another mother who was making a big fuss of wanting to be home to her other child, they were assuring her the baby needed the extra care and that was more important. She should be patient like I was they said – I liked that.

Sheila and Les came to visit with Tony and Christopher who loved seeing his new baby brother.

There was some sadness while in Rinteln knowing a baby boy born the day before Stuart had lost his Mummy as he was born, like Stuart he was in special care. I noted some of the nurses were more tender with him than others. I think often of that now young man and wonder how life has been for him.

After two weeks we were able to go home with some follow up checkups to attend. Stuart was a very good baby in those first weeks, letting us all settle in well.

Chris came in lots and we could sit together feeding our babies while Christopher and Tony played. Our men were so often away, so Chris and I spent so much time together taking our children on many adventures finding new play areas and often getting lost, Chris always blamed me. I know my lack of sense of direction was true but she was there too! On one particular day we chose to take a short cut through a cemetery and couldn't find a way out, we walked for miles making it a lot later than we intended getting back, luckily with our men away it didn't matter too much. With the children tired out they were ready for a quick supper and bed. This was the pattern of how we spent the next four years, plenty of great walks. Christopher, Stuart, Tony and Natalie were such good friends together even if on any walks where there was water or mud about, Tony was always the one who fell in and got wet or muddy, it was quite funny.

Stuart and Natalie were christened together. Chris and I prepared an elaborate buffet held in Tony and my flat. It was such an enjoyable afternoon, all our friends from the estate joined us and had such a good time they decided after they had put their children to bed they would come back in the evening and did just that, it was really nice.

At other times we had the wives' club to attend, to include outings now and then – at one time to a pottery factory. I remember Chris laughing at me as said 'I was the smallest person who bought the biggest pot'. We had seen these being made and I loved it. There were trips out for Mums and children when the men were away for longer to various venues. One time we went to Potts Park, we had to bring our own picnic, of course, Chris and I made sure we wouldn't starve with too much food! That day Tony again managed to spill orange juice over his tee shirt Chris having to get it off quickly as wasps were surrounding him, poor Tony, we had a laugh! So there was really lots going on or we would just enjoy walks through the wood on our estate and round the lake or letting the children play outdoors while we sat chatting with other Mums.

I was delighted to hear that Betty, Brian and Gordon were going to come for a holiday and Tony decided to buy a car so that we could enjoy trips out. Betty loved our flat. They arrived early afternoon, Gordon was around eleven years old, we had a walk through the wood and round the lake. Tony went to collect our car the next day though as there was a serious thunder storm; I worried till he got home safely.

It was very exciting as we went for some great drives, found a bird park to enjoy, took them to Herman's Dankmal Monument and a bird of prey sanctuary in the most glorious setting. Having the car made such a difference, we enjoyed revisiting these places with Chris, John, Tony and Natalie.

Another time Sheila and Les, Tony's parents, came with his Aunt and Uncle, that was very nice, though Sheila and Iris did have some fall outs as they were known to do over the years. We also had Chris, Eric, Marianne and Lee again, it was great to have them and show them our life in Germany. Greta was another visitor; it was always nice looking forward to visitors.

Chris and I thought it would be nice to have a holiday so decided on the Black Forest and began to make plans. We booked a Eurocamp holiday where tents were set up ready and with four young children, we needed plenty of luggage. After we'd made plans John wasn't able to come with us so Chris's sister Della said she would come over from Luton. There was no way we would all fit in the car. Chris and I thought it would be nice for the six of us to travel on the train, the children would love that, and Tony and Della, with our car very full of luggage, were going to drive and be there ahead of us to set up camp!

We enjoyed our journey though not speaking German was no help when the train stopped in the middle of our journey and everyone got off letting us know to do the same, not understanding why, but to leave our bags. Later I was to learn Chris was very impressed with how calmly I reacted to all this. After some minutes the train had moved and came back and we all got on again, very confusing! It was fine, we got there to see Tony and Della settled in our two tents. We enjoyed the holiday very much, the kiddies loved running round and enjoyed the barbeques. We had one under the awning as it had rained. Natalie, who was only three like Stuart, befriended some of the German campers returning with ice lollies or sweets, and rather loved the hand dryers in the toilets. What a character, we had to watch her, she did indeed get lost one day and had us all searching for her. It was there we renamed the Willow tree as Christopher called it – the 'baggy tree.' Tony, myself, Christopher and Stuart drove to Bern, Chris didn't want to come that day, it was a super outing. I compared the main street to London's Regent Street. We came back with 'goodies' from the Lindt sweet shop. We went for some great walks in the Black Forest, climbs too, enjoying a tea shop after a climb and then an almost roll down a very steep hill and through some fields of sweet corn to get back to camp. We went up a mountain on a chair lift; enjoying lovely views and Tony at only four saying are we going in the pub later! One of the nicest days out was to Titisee, it was so perfect, a great clock shop, a magnificent lake, I loved it, we had a great boat trip. I think everyone enjoyed the holiday, all too soon it was over and we packed up ready for home, no adventure on the train journey this time.

Chris and I continued to enjoy great walks with our children finding really nice areas for them to play in. We were always out and about, I loved her company, she reminded me of Joan and the great times we had together.

Tony, Natalie, Christopher and Stuart were really good friends, those were very relaxed years to enjoy before our children were into school years. I loved being a Mummy and so enjoyed life at Amposteich.

Hilary and Joe, who had recently married, came to live near us, Tony knew Joe and invited them over for an evening with us. We loved their company and became good friends, we had many serious discussions and laughs at Hilary's very strong views on many aspects of life. She was very firm that she didn't want to have children and strong opinions on equal partnership in marriage, me saying to Tony – Hilary wouldn't pick up your socks and pants from the floor! We had some laughs and enjoyed friendly dinner parties together, I liked them both very much.

The Summer Ball was always a great event to enjoy once we had sorted out baby sitters and, of course, ball gowns. They were very high class evenings creating some fun times.

Christopher was ready to start play school in the camp, I hated to see him cry on that first day, leaving his Mummy. He came home with a picture he'd painted and soon got used to it.

It was nice to have their sports day and to see Christopher in a lovely blue velour suit which his Nanny and Granddad had bought him. Stuart was very shy with everyone, it was important to get him to mix with people.

There was a special function for Tony's squadron so Chris agreed to baby sit for us. This was near to the end of our tour in Germany and we were more or less packed up for our move. The evening was great, I had a really nice chat with Captain Payne, Tony's boss, and Rose who worked in their office. They were full of praise for Tony, he was so good at his job, I was loving hearing this. They did say it was very important for Tony to take his Maths and English exams to enable him to be promoted.

We had promised Chris we wouldn't be late, I somehow got carried away forgetting the time, though did protest when at the end Rose wanted us all at her flat, no one had listened to me and we were driven there where we were served with champagne and orange juice though just one, not the best idea and we were rather late home. Poor Chris was rightly not pleased and rushed off home as we came in. Next day I bought her some flowers and a vase as means of 'an olive branch' and of course she forgave me. That day as they looked out the windows in her flat Stuart got his arm stuck between the radiator and the wooden window sill. It was hard to free him as the radiator was hot, he had a small nasty burn just above his elbow. We cooled it as best we could. Chris had been a nurse and knew how to best cool it till we could take him to the medical centre. Stuart still holds the scar from that burn to this day. It was hard to believe our time in Germany had almost come to an end. Our boxes were packed and en route. We were left preparing for the handover of our flat, this was a major event as it had to be immaculate. Any faults led to charges, many of the well schooled wives were up to all the tricks, I'd hear of brown polish to hide scratches, coloured crayons to conceal radiator marks on the carpet and many more. I was lucky with Tony as he was always so particular, taking the cooker to bits to ensure it was completely clean, taps, too, unscrewed to ensure left blemish free, he was very good.

We travelled by coach to Gutersloh, then our flight to Luton 'Chris's home town' and coach to Windsor. It was a long and tiring day for the children, us too as it was late and dark when we arrived in Windsor for refreshments before collecting the key to our new home and getting the coach for the short trip. I hadn't lived on Broom Farm before and as it was dark, it was lucky that I had Chris to guide the boys and I to the right block. Tony was not with us as he had the car journey and boat to Dover. He was to stay with his Mum and Dad in Ramsgate that night. The house felt cold and not as impressive as when we arrived at our Amposteich flat.

Chapter 18

Windsor

The next morning we were able to explore our new home and area. Tony arrived back with us in the early hours of the morning, he was eager to get to our new home and didn't stay at his Mum and Dad's as planned.

Christopher was ready to start school and Stuart had a nursery place there too. Alexander School was on the estate and Mrs Davies was the headmistress.

We all settled into our new routine; Chris lived a few doors up from us.

It was very funny one day as we took the bus to town, Stuart saw a nun get on, he turned to me and said 'Mummy is that the Queen?' I was about to answer but Christopher beat me to it and said 'don't be silly that's baby Jesus's Mother,' I thought it was lovely.

I started to look for a part time job and Jan my next door neighbour said there was work at a very small factory next to our estate, not really my kind of work, but so near and the hours were perfect. I was lucky to get the job, this was a factory making hose type tubing, it was a small team and quite pleasant. We even got some overtime during the summer months. The owners were very kind and treated us to a lovely meal at Christmas and a nice bonus.

That job lasted for eighteen months before the factory closed, by this time Stuart was also at school. It meant that I could work some more hours. This time I was determined to get back into kitchen work and was lucky to find a job in the kitchen of a residential home in Old Windsor, a bit of a distance from home. I wasn't actually cooking but helping in the kitchen, it was a very strange job, the Chef wasn't very good and I noted a supposedly discreet relationship between him and Gail his assistant.

At Christmas, Matron hated the way he had iced the cake and wanted it redone. Gail felt she couldn't do it so it was left to me. We got over that and the job continued for just over eighteen months when The Manor was going to close down. A shame, the manor house was in beautiful grounds.

I did manage to get another kitchen job, this time in a pub kitchen right next to Windsor Castle. It was very popular, our team: Sue, the cook; Marilyn and I assistants; and Joe to wash up. Sue was a big girl with serious mood swings and seemed to take an instant dislike to me, I feel because she noted that I had a good knowledge of cooking; she was a very strange girl. Mario and Judy were the owners, they were really nice, The Carpenters Arms was a busy pub.

I gave them some recipe ideas that became popular, not pleasing Sue, and I put up with it for a time. One day the atmosphere was so bad with Sue's moods you could hear everyone breathe. When I went down to our cellar stock room I told Mario, he called her out and had a word with her. That year at Christmas I hung back to have a word with her as I handed her a Christmas gift asking just what exactly her problem was with me. Sue got the shock of her life and from that day on was totally different, we 'almost' became friends. I can do it if I'm sure I'm right, it paid off. That next Christmas she gave me the most lovely pair of earrings. She was to be married to Ian. I'd never ever seen her dressed other than in jeans and plain tops. The dress she chose for her wedding was so lovely. I forgave the earlier resentment and gave her a superb wedding gift. Life was more relaxed at the pub now, I was enjoying it. Chris, an elderly lady, a friend of Judy's, came in to help now and then, she and I became friends.

The boys were enjoying school. I had to be very sure to be home in time especially for Stuart, he hated me to be late and it worried and upset him. He suffered from a lack of confidence sadly, taking after me. I would never have wanted that for him it, can hold you back so much.

When first in Windsor everyone commented on how Stuart was always right at Christopher's shadow, again I'm sure a confidence thing, though I was so pleased to see him grow in esteem as he got relaxed to life on the estate. I loved seeing the difference in him, gradually having his own friends and enjoying life. We had a small back yard, behind that a field where they played and had lots of fun.

At Christmas each year Tony's artistic talent came to full use. We had a nice kitchen window where he created wonderful scenes, over the years much admired by all who passed our window, he really went to great lengths to get it right to meet his high standards.

During this period one of our fondest family memories has to be the days we walked in the woods or Windsor Great Park to find the right branch for our Christmas tree. For this we loved tramping through high ferns or crunchy wood floor coverings, that day felt very special to me as one we all so much enjoyed, coming home exhausted but delighted. Tony would let our branch dry then spray it in our chosen colour, often white. It would then be hung on our wall and decorated, always looking so special, our home was never ordinary over the Christmas period.

I feel proud to know our boys were brought up in a loving happy home with the greatest love and care we could give them.

One day on our way to the Naafi we met in with Tony who said to me 'Auntie Alice why don't you visit so much now?' I said 'it's different now to Germany we all have to get ready for school and are kept busy,' he then said 'my Mum's having a baby!'

I called in later to see Chris she confirmed 'yes' she was pregnant again and not all that pleased about it for a while.

There was a request for army wives and children to take part in an exercise at Salisbury Plain so Chris and I put our names forward to take part, we were told we act as evacuees at the outbreak of war – sounds like fun!

The day came and we travelled by coach. Near to our venue we saw some parachute jumpers, there were comments of 'hope we're not expected to do that' I thought so too! I could feel my lack of confidence and wondered what lay ahead this weekend.

On arrival we were given a talk on how things were to be, then lined up to be signed in. It was at this time Chris chose to play a prank on me, letting it be known to officials she thought I may be a spy! Chris loved a laugh! Those comments resulted in myself, Christopher and Stuart being segregated from the others and led off first to be searched then imprisoned. We were led to an enclosed location in a guarded area where we were given cups of tea in tin mugs. I don't think the boys knew what to think of it all – I'm not sure I did either, my goodness Chris that's one payback I owe you! We were moved to yet another enclosure, more tea and plenty of waiting. Eventually we were to be reunited with the rest of our evacuees. We had a short trip in a Chinook to see everyone in the food tent. Chris was laughing so hard as we joined them though she too admitted concern at what she'd caused, we had a good laugh over it all and went to eat. It had been quite a long day so it was a walk to the toilets then a horrid communal basin for teeth cleaning before going to our marquee where there were so many floor mattresses ready for us. Christopher, Stuart and I were right under a bulbous dent in the tent roof that was filled with water, I prayed it would hold and not burst or leak, it would have been very cold. The children were so tired they slept, but it was very noisy with sounds of continuous helicopters, tanks and people about, what a night that was! We'd just all sort of settled, I knew I would never sleep, when serious noise erupted and we heard a familiar sound 'crash out, crash out!' Caroline Steele, one of our friends, shouted out 'be quiet we're trying to get some sleep!' Of course them all dashing around at great speed they took no notice. More so while we lived in Germany we had got to know of these crash outs that could be at any time, often in the middle of the night, all the soldiers having to get to their posts in record time. Our last day of the exercise was to have breakfast and get ready to leave, we were taken back to base in a Hercules, such a massive plane and the back was open. Christopher was sick, he helped himself to a big breakfast, it was a great experience, but I was glad that it was a short trip, then we were settled into our coach for Windsor. By this time both boys were sick, I didn't feel that well myself, plenty of us on the coach felt the same way. Back at barracks Tony was there to meet us and I gave him the sick bags to dispose of before we took two very tired young boys and their very tired Mum home.

The whole weekend was a great adventure I wouldn't have missed for anything. I remember standing in the Post Office queue next day, still tired, but thinking to myself 'you wouldn't believe what we've been through this weekend!'

Some weeks later we all got a letter from the barracks thanking us for taking part in a successful exercise.

Chris's husband John was to be posted to Bovington and they would move to Dorset, still this wasn't until after their third baby's birth.

Tony's birthday was the 1st of November, Chris' was the day before October 31st. They had always made much issue over this in Germany, Tony saying his was 'All Saints Day', Chris at Halloween, and now her baby was due on the same day . Chris said 'I don't want a shared birthday', but as it turned out Richard came into our world on the 1st November, Tony's birthday. Chris asked Tony and I to be his Godparents, they would have moved before it was time for his christening, we assured Chris that we would make the trip to be there for that event.

Stuart suffered a lot with sore throats and had glandular fever at one time. He was very brave when he had to have blood taken, that is till we had a hospital appointment and a young nurse really messed up taking some blood having to have two or three attempts, I was cross over that as it shouldn't have happened. He had some time off school, and me off work, then he was not able to take part in any football or sport for a set time till well again. This was hard for Stuart as he loved sport of all kinds.

We did go to Richard's christening, it was nice to see them all again. Christopher missed Tony at school as even the teachers noted their friendship, reminding me on how they had been listening in on a conversation the two of them were having on the coach on a school trip them telling us they were really funny.

We had enjoyed a day in Poole on our way to Chris and John's, visiting a sea life centre. That day Tony and boys had a photo taken with a Boa Constrictor snake round their necks, a certain 'no' from me to join them.

The christening was lovely we all enjoyed the day being together again, I did miss having Chris nearby.

It was nice being in Windsor as we were nearer to Betty and Brian for them to visit or us to visit them. Tony's Mum and Dad came now and then, Sheila, my Mum in law, liked the shops in Windsor, of course, we also liked to visit them in Ramsgate sometimes.

Terry, who I always kept in touch with, came to see us at one time and took Tony and I out for a lovely meal in Eton. Our only problem with Terry's visits is that once he started having drinks he sometimes forgot to stop! Terry wanted to treat Tony and I, Christopher and Stuart to enjoy a nice meal out in London, we could manage for a night at his flat.

His choice of restaurant was always very high class, having served at Clarence House for twenty three years he had seen firsthand how things should be done, it did rub off, he liked it that way. Each year around Christmas we enjoyed a wonderful meal at The St John's Wood Hilton, The Regent Palace Hotel or The Cumberland. Terry's health was not very good, his nerves were bad, his eyesight was not good, our elderly waiter looked after us so well. Terry could almost be an embarrassment in his ways though meant well. He had let the waiter know exactly how he liked to be looked after. We must indeed have made ourselves very memorable as the next Christmas we went to another superb restaurant, and the following year we went back to The Cumberland and recognised the same waiter. That day he was working in the bar, that was until Terry realised it was him and insisted he would look after us; he was really nice and did just that. He remembered us well, astonishing me after two years and all the people he must have served, I found it very funny. Terry's eye sight was much worse now and he really needed the looking after he insisted on having, I did sort of apologise for Terry's demands. He understood and was very kind as could see how bad Terry's nerves were, he sat and chatted with us for a while, telling us of his life and that he was now in his last working year, he was a nice person. Terry was very generous with his tips, to me it still seemed amusingly bizarre he had remembered us two years on when working in a busy London restaurant, we really must have made an impression.

Stuart really loved football and had become a staunch Liverpool supporter from when he was really young; we noted he had a love for all sport. He now had a small group of his own friends and became more independent from Christopher.

We did as much as we could to help support the school to raise money, they sold home-made cakes and biscuits on Fridays. It must have been Easter when I impressed Mrs Davies with a chicken shaped cake. Tony had iced this for me, it looked really good he was always so exact, little did I realise how this talent of his would be so helpful to my work in future years.

When Tony's Mum and Dad came for a weekend and they had all been out to a garden centre I was shocked when they came home with a new pet they had bought for Tony. A tarantula spider! Not my idea of a family pet, though I knew Tony had always wanted one. I could learn to live with that, this would not have been the case if it had been a snake, I wouldn't have let them in! That was another pet he liked... We called our spider 'Chile' as was his country of origin, we also had a cockatiel. Stuart named him Noddy. Both pets became much loved and so well looked after.

Christopher loved playing soldier games with his friends, we noted how he always pleaded with his Dad to drive past the barracks, they both loved riding their bikes around the estate.

We did have one major incident and all had to evacuate our homes as there was a bomb scare! At first we went over to a new garden centre opposite our homes while the bomb squad were there, it lasted so long the boys and I went to my friend Chris, who I worked at the pub with, and we had our supper with her while we waited for the all clear. Tony came to collect us, the silly part of this it was a hoax caused by an army couple who had fallen out and for some reason the wife had taped something under the car, I can't imagine why!

This wasn't our only touch of adventure, while at Broom Farm, as while the men were away on exercise we were all left in the dark due to a major and serious power cut that was to last over four days, it was quite good fun actually to see how we managed with no gas or electric, we read stories by candle light, made tea boiling the water on my fondue pot, Jan next door saying 'Alice could I have a bit of water for some tea' in her nice Irish accent, we had some laughs, a good job it was summer and no heating needed. Shirley, one of our wives, managed to open the Naafi for us, having to use a cash box as no tills could be used, it was quite good fun all pulling together. This was caused by a major fire at a power station.

Christopher and Jan's Kerry-Anne often played nicely together, all of them sometimes played on the field behind our houses, playing shops or book sales. It was nice to see them enjoy play while some of us wives sat and had cups of tea in the field. There were many good times and some not so good of course, children fight now and then even parents fall out. I was very cross at one Mum as I heard her swear at my Stuart, I told her 'I don't use language like that to my children and don't expect you to'. She didn't take it well becoming very abusive telling me stories of my Tony in his younger years, she wasn't even there, so out of order, of course that was a big fall out for us, I just ignored her, I was never normally involved in ugly disputes this was very much not my way. It was some months later at our Summer Ball that she came over and placed a drink in front of me, saying 'for you Alice', her way of an apology.

In Tony's job he was often called to put up marquees for various events, the boys loved to go and help him do this as they always had great fun and were sometimes very spoiled. One of these times was for a caravan club who invited us to join them for the evening, we did that and had such a great time. Another time was at St Margaret's Hospital in Windsor, the day Christopher had got a plastic tie stuck on his wrist and Tony had to get a nurse to cut it off! Or the time they had a lovely day erecting a tent and stayed at the function. I was shocked to learn that Stuart had been trusted to go over and give a bag of money, Tony said four hundred pounds, to someone in authority, they both loved it all, I expect I was at work some of those days.

We were all enjoying life in Windsor and boys were really growing up now, each with their own special personality. Soon Christopher would go on to middle school which was not on our estate.

At one time when Tony was away I decided to take the boys to visit Mrs Davidson, they were only six and seven or so, we chose to travel through the day from Kings Cross to Aberdeen and then another train on to Inverurie. I was well prepared for the long journey with eats and drinks and a little surprise every two hours such as pack of soldiers, colouring books and crayons, small cars or me reading to them. It was a superb journey and they were good as gold, it worked perfectly, we were so lucky our last train was there, no waiting. We enjoyed our days, Mrs Davidson's son Bob came round, the boys helped him gather up the potatoes he had dug up in her garden, they loved that, I took them out to play areas, it was very nice, they slept on the bed settee in the living room while Mrs Davidson and I sat by the window with lights off for the boys, we chatted lit by the street lamp. Mr Davidson had died the year before, I felt sad as she talked of his last illness and his passing, both of us with tears running down our cheeks. I so wanted to reach over and hug her, I still didn't have the confidence to do so somehow feeling it wasn't my place, silly I know as I really cared so very much for her and felt her pain. That had been the reason I wanted to visit.

The next day the boys and I were going to stay with Chris and Eric for a couple of days. Marianne and Lee seemed so grown up now, they had a lovely little dog Lucy and the boys loved her. Chris and I stayed up till late at night to catch up with all our news, it was always lovely being with them. The next day Chris said Christopher showed her up when she had said to Lucy 'I'll feed you in a minute' Christopher said 'it will only take a minute Auntie Chris!' I expect we were tired after our late night, we laughed over that moment. Our next visit was to Bunty's for a couple of days, she enjoyed having the boys; she lived on her own now since our Mum had died. Bunty had given up work a little ahead of her retirement to look after our Mum in her last years, of course we sat and talked of our Mum, I don't ever think Bunty fully understood how difficult some of the years we had gone through while growing up had been, even though she and Mary had visited us now and then.

We were in Germany when our mother had died, I was sorry really I couldn't fly home to Scotland, Stuart was only a few months old and, as still being seen by a specialist, I wouldn't risk the chance of him being ill, all the rest of the family were there, I really did so much want to be with them. The night of our mother's death Bunty was at her bedside and could hear the Armistice service being played on the television in the ward, it was as 'The Last Post' was being played our mother was taking her last breaths, a memory that would forever stay with Bunty on hearing that piece of music. Bunty had stayed on at our Mum's house.

As we spent our last day at Bunty's Geordie called in to visit, it was lovely to see him and he insisted he would drive us to Mary and Willie in Aberdeen, first we were to call in at his home to tell his wife Doris, it was nice to see their home and enjoy a cup of tea with them. Geordie took the boys to the milking shed to see the cows, they liked that, then he drove us to Aberdeen to spend the night with Mary and Willie before our trip back to London, then Windsor. Mary told us that they had a visit from Betty, Brian and Gordon before our holiday. Mary said 'how will Alice manage to travel all that way with two such young boys!' Brian's reply had been 'oh don't you worry Alice will manage very well indeed I'm sure of that', so thank you Brian, hearing that I felt was a nice compliment.

That visit had been when I was younger and we had not long come back from Germany.

The boys were older now and Christopher was ready to start at middle school, he and Kerry-Anne walked together there as this was not on our estate, once settled they enjoyed the bigger school. We attended a great musical concert there one evening, it was our regiment The Life Guards Band who were playing, there was to be a sponsored walk at the school, Christopher was eager to join in, his teacher Mrs Duncan said they were very short of helpers, on hearing this Tony and his Friend Jim were happy to help, the weather was perfect everyone loved the day, it was a long walk, Tony had taken some photos they turned out very well Christopher showed them to Mrs Duncan who wanted some copies for herself.

Stuart had only just started at middle school, doing just one term, before the time came for us to go back to Germany, I had to hand in my notice at The Carpenters Arms and make ready for our move.

Having lived in Germany before it wasn't quite the ordeal it had been last time, still it was a new place, a new time and a whole new adventure for us to look forward to.

Chapter 19

Kavallerie Weg

Once more we were taken to our new home after refreshment at Atholone Barracks. It was on quite a small estate and, I felt, lacked the wonderful setting of our Amposteich home. It was rather strange to find the flat was almost an exact replica, though much older and in a way more shabby, it made me feel a bit flat and sad and of course no Chris this time.

It was very different this time, our boys were older and would be collected by bus each day for school.

As soon as we'd settled Tony took me to Horrocks Barracks where I put my name in an agency to find work and almost before I felt ready the boys came home one day with a letter from Mr Hoyle, their school bursar, for me to call in to see him. I felt my lack of confidence come to the fore again and almost didn't want it, but of course I did go and left no time to change my mind as he had me start work on the Monday, at 7am. This was my start of life at John Buchan School where my boys attended, now I would too.

It was a long walk to our estate, I was very concerned when told that two of us would cook three hundred meals, it was even worse that there were some facts he didn't tell me! On Monday I met Andrea, the cook, who said she did first course and I was to do desserts. There was a team of eight ladies, the others coming in at later stages, two who did all the vegetables and potatoes, the other four washing up and cleaning, four of us to serve up lunches.

The kitchen was vast and really great to work with in some aspects. The big gas cookers, bain marie and bratwurst pans, I hadn't used before, and the two big boilers, walk in fridge and a lovely long serving hatch, it all felt enormous and rather scary. What Mr Hoyle hadn't told me was that Andrea was working her last week before their posting back to England, I only found out on my second day when I hadn't even settled in! Those first days were hard. I found my shoes weren't right for the flooring – it felt very slippery and lethal, one time I slipped and fell, hitting my arm on a lever for gas supply, the next day I had an enormous bruise on my arm. Tony was very concerned to see that, so the right shoes were top priority.

The next week I was to have my interview at Horrocks Barracks, it seemed strange after already having worked for a week, but Mr Hoyle was keen for me to take head cook job. I lacked confidence and chose to be second cook, of course I got the job and on the Monday I met Rose, our new cook, we each worked at our own steel top table opposite each other. We had some nice chats together before the other staff came in, but of course there was a bit of rivalry between us. Rose was mother of four children and some years younger than I was, we mostly got on, but I have to say we did have our moments.

There were some very different ways to get used to, like how I had to make the custard or rice in this big boiler that used to get scalding hot – one touch on the edge left me with plenty of burn marks. The thing that amused me was the broom handle with a whisk on the end of it that I had to use to make the custard, it was very difficult till I got the knack of it and soon managed to make the perfect custard I had always achieved. When I really settled in I began to enjoy work at John Buchan, it was nice to get to know the other ladies, though I do feel that eight ladies working together can lead to some personality clashes, as I noted the frictions that arose sometimes that I could see no reason for. Once I got used to it all I was proud to know I was getting great feedback and my skills noted as I added to the menu. Mr Hoyle decided that we should change places once a month; I think it was good for both of us, though Rose wasn't too impressed at first. We got on well together in a guarded way; Rose had been in catering school, she didn't like it too much to see the acclaim I gained with some dishes that were much favoured both here and I could use in all my future employments, such as when I made vegetable curry to my own recipe. This was much loved, we had many vegetarians, it created quite an atmosphere as they seemed to come over individually to thank me, I felt quite proud and it was very good for my confidence. That particular dish was being talked of outside school as teachers were entitled to use the Officers mess and they spoke of it there and I was further elated when a top chef asked if he could have my recipes as he'd heard so much of chicken curry, quiches, casseroles and gravies, all were given equal acclaim, I did love all these comments. In truth we were very fortunate in B.F.P.O. schools as they always used fresh meats and produce, very different as I would discover to school kitchens back home.

Christopher and Stuart settled in well at school, I loved to see Stuart was so enjoying life at Kavallerie Weg. He was making friends and so involved in all sport, he loved it, it was so good for him. Christopher, we noted, was taking a great interest in history, he too was enjoying life. When at home they both played outdoors almost all the time, it was nice to see them loving life so much. When the season for any sport was on the boys were always involved, even when we had a very late snow one year and it was very cold they played out and had so much fun. Like the time a group of them had arranged what was considered a very important football match. This was between two different estates, ours were the 'Kavallerie Kickers' against the 'Dragooners' from Dragoon Weg. We were very amused, it was all taken so seriously, I can't even think who won, but we loved the enthusiasm of it all. I love my Stuart oh so much, that love is there for life and beyond, I hope he can feel it always.

Christopher was a little less shy had a great enthusiasm for anything he was involved in, he too gained in confidence and ability, though had to work hard to achieve his goals, his school reports were always fairly good, though I did worry over his spelling and writing, needlessly as it turned out as the determination to achieve his aims was there in abundance. I also want Christopher to know of my lifetime love for him in this life and beyond. My boys mean everything to me.

One day we made the journey back to our old home in Amposteich to let our boys see where we'd lived on our first tour of Germany and we had a walk around the wood I had so enjoyed when they were so young.

That awoke so many memories of our time there, the fun walks with Chris, Tony and Natalie, the nights there were 'crash outs,' to have loud knocks on the door to get a speedy response from the soldiers getting to the barracks at fastest possible time, often we had just settled back to sleep to hear more door knocking someone else checking our men had gone. It was a nightmare but fun now to look back on, to see the estate come alive with lights on while the men got ready to go. We had this happen so many times while in Germany.

Tony worked in H.Q. Squadron, he was well thought of and took great pride in his work, the ammunition store was one of his responsibilities. His most hated job was when he was on night guard duty, as I expect it was for most of them.

This time while in Germany all security had to be stepped up as it was the start of the Gulf War, this created a whole different atmosphere. I did feel fortunate that as Tony was in H.Q. Squadron he didn't go to war; it was a very busy time for everyone.

At work a place was available for one person to take a course to gain an intermediate food handling course, Rose was asked but didn't want it, so I agreed to take the place. I was nervous and wondered what I'd let myself in for, I had never been a great scholar. This was a three month course before an exam both oral and written… 'oh help!' I had classes to attend at the barracks, this was with all the army chefs and three ladies. I enjoyed the course and had no problem passing the oral part, sure enough the written part took a second attempt from me but I did pass on the retake and was delighted to have both my basic and intermediate food handler's certificates. I felt quite proud of myself to have gained this prestigious award and knew it would help me in any future employment I applied for.

Rose and I had a bit of a fallout during the time of working for my certificate as one day I saw her make what I felt was a really dangerous move. She had prepared liver for part of lunch menu and went on to prepare the cold meat tray, I was very alarmed to note she hadn't cleared up after the raw meat. I thought before I spoke but felt I really had to say the danger she was creating, of course she didn't like it and retaliated saying that I wasn't perfect. I'm sure I wasn't but I couldn't not have mentioned it. Rose went off in a huff for her tea break; my ears were burning, I never bothered with the break as most of them smoked, I liked that quiet half hour. Rose calmed down from her fury, we got over it, I told her I wasn't being nasty but protecting our jobs and everyone's health. If the catering health officer had come in we may both have lost our jobs. Rose did say she understood and apologised for her reaction so we put it behind us. Rose was difficult but could be very kind, now and then she gave me a lift home to save me the three quarter hour walk that I normally did.

At Christmas we were so busy, we cooked twelve fresh turkeys and had them all to carve, a massive task, but we did it together. I loved to make spectacular gravy with the carcasses in the brat pans, it was perfect, I made sure I made it as I didn't like Rose's gravy.

I loved some of the compliments and comments I received from the school and to have the daughter of one soldier who was talking with Tony, on realising he was my husband, to have her say 'oh you're married to the lady with the sweet voice!' I liked it when Tony told me that, or to have met a young lad, now left our school, come over to me while shopping in Schloss Neuhaus and say how much he missed my cooking, I thought that so lovely.

There was a cook's job coming up at The Robert Browning Primary School and I was told that if I walked into the office in Barracks school and say you want it, the job is yours with no interview. Very complimentary I thought, but I liked the fact we had a more varied menu, theirs would have been set and limited, so chose not to take the offer.

Tony and I made some new friends, Tony's work colleagues actually, and he wanted to invite them to our home for dinner. Ken and his German wife Agatha came, we had a very enjoyable evening and continued to be friends together. They had a nice big flat near to our school, together with the boys we spent some happy times with them and with Ken and Agatha in our company for the Summer Ball at the barracks.

We still had times with Tony away on exercise and night time crash outs, you never knew what to expect.

There was a barracks sports day when much to my horror we were included in the family fun race, not my kind of thing really. That day we sat with Captain Slater, Tony's boss, I could feel he took to me, always after, I knew my thoughts were right and when Tony took ill after a B.F.T. (fitness test) he came to the school to collect me from work and on to see Tony, he did spend a few days in hospital but was soon well and home again.

Tony came home one day telling me that there were offers of redundancy and he did think this might be a good time to accept as the boys were almost ready for senior school and would have had to travel a long journey there. They had even asked us if we had thoughts on allowing our children to be weekly boarders, I had very firmly replied 'no' to that idea, I wanted to bring my children up, I wouldn't have accepted that.

I wasn't sure if I was pleased at the idea of Tony accepting redundancy but I did see the sense in what he was saying so his choice was right for us.

One evening, as we sat at home, a telegram was delivered from my brother Bill to let us know Mrs Davidson had died, I felt very low and devastated, I hadn't realised she had been in hospital for three weeks. For many years she had suffered with heart problems and had given up her home, spending time with each of her six children before finally settling to live with her son Jim and his wife Nan.

I had only just had a week off for half term and would have chosen to visit her in hospital that week, it wasn't an easy choice but I decided not to fly home for her funeral. Of course I sent flowers and wrote to the family. I knew I would miss her friendship and our letters to each other.

Soon it was time for us to start to make our plans for our life out of the army. It was a bit scary to feel we were getting ready to start a whole new life, especially having not really any set plans for our future.

Tony decided we would first live in Dover as would be near to his parents and his sister Theresa and her family.

I was now so well settled in my work I felt quite sad that I would soon be leaving.

It felt all too soon we were getting our boxes packed ready for our move. Ken and Agatha took Tony and I out for a meal in their favourite restaurant, as well as to invite us along with Christopher and Stuart to dine with them on our last night in Germany. The girls at work had arranged a party for me at

Rose's house the day I finished work at the school. In some ways I felt sad to leave, though excited to start on our future plans.

The very last day, and we had completed our house handover and were pleased that went with no charges as I knew it would with Tony's input, he knew how exact everything had to be.

We were going on to Tony's friend Jimmy till our time for leaving, we had our pets in the car, our tarantula and cockatiel, all correct certificates gained to bring them into Britain. We had to do the same for the houseplants that went with our furniture.

That night was unforgettable as we drove through Germany. There was a major football match on the radio between Liverpool and... I forget the other team name. We were desperate for Liverpool to win not to have Stuart upset, it even went to penalties and yes they won and we could relax with our contented son.

The Taft family are on their way home.

We arrived at the port and felt lucky to be given special treatment as we had already informed them a pet spider was to be carried on board, the customs officers were keen to see Chile in our car, they then gave us a special escort first on to the ferry.

We could now settle for our crossing, I thought back to that last night in the flat with our home ready for handover, we had mattresses on the living room floor to sleep on. That night there was an earthquake felt throughout parts of Germany, we felt the tremor, quite a memory.

As we saw The White Cliffs of Dover get nearer, to know that this was the start of a whole new chapter in our lives, I did wonder what the future would hold for us.

As it was Friday we were going to Ramsgate to stay with Tony's Mum and Dad for a few days till Tony could collect the keys for our temporary home in the now disused Old Park Barracks.

Sheila and Les, Tony's Mum and Dad, were very excited at our home coming and their neighbour Paula had a beautifully iced cake to welcome us. I loved Sheila and Les, we had great friendship together and they loved having their grandsons back home so that we could see them more often, this would be the first time we had ever lived so near to them, his sister Theresa lived in Margate.

Some days later we got the keys and moved to our new home, it felt very strange to live in an almost empty barracks with only a few houses occupied. The boys liked it, there was plenty of space for them to use their bikes. The house was a bit too small and we had to put some of our furniture in storage. Tony was on leave now and still paid for six months, it was important that we started to plan for our future. I was lucky to find a job as cook in a residential home, though knew this was temporary, while we started to look for a permanent home. I loved house hunting, I was a bit fussy, not liking places that were litter strewn, one of my pet hates. We did view quite a lot of properties in different areas of Dover till eventually Tony found the house we live in till this day, the area was peaceful and quiet and within easy reach of the town. It was very exciting to feel we would have our own home after more than fourteen years in army accommodation.

We hadn't got the keys by the time I came home from work one day to be met with a big surprise, I walked in to see my lovely sister Mary and husband Willie sitting on the settee, we had no word of their visit, it was delightful. They had been on a coach trip holiday that took them to Canterbury for one night. It was so lovely to see them, I was just sorry we didn't have the keys to show them what was to be our home, it had to be a very short visit, but I loved it.

I was looking out for a cook's job in a school as working hours were perfect for the boys to have me home with them and the same holidays. I was lucky to get an interview and soon given a school near to our new home. The house was up a hill, the school even more so, wow it was steep! It was a big secondary school and so very different from Germany in every way. My job started at the beginning of the term just as we were making our house ready to move into.

It was such a lovely time doing up the house, we were lucky having the two homes during this time. Tony had found work on a temporary basis so he and his Dad worked hard in the house every weekend, Les was so happy working with his son, I could see how much pleasure it gave him, it was a delight. They almost gutted the house to make it ready for us, there was lots to do before furnishing time. One weekend we decided to have a break from work on the house, I phoned Sheila and Les, I could hear his disappointment not to be working that weekend.

It was hard getting used to work at this school, I felt it wasn't really right for me. Though everyone felt the food was very good there were a lot of issues: no proper serving hatch, the kitchen was poor, the muddle at serving time – these were young adults all taller than me, not middle school kids, most had heavy bags to carry round even to their lunchtime. The food counter was so poor it annoyed me, after a few months I was going to leave and told the management, they offered me a different school so I agreed to give it a try.

We moved into our new house, it felt so nice to have it all fresh and to our own choice with our furniture back out of storage.

My new school was a bit further but I could still walk, the boys' school was further for them too but they could take a bus. They had settled in quite well at Archers Court School and began to make some new friends.

I arrived at St Mary's School with nothing more than an idea of what was expected of me, there was no one about as it was early morning, I had to first find the office to be given the keys and direction of the kitchen, there was no clue to be found of what was for lunch or idea of numbers. 'Oh help' I thought and looked in the freezer where I found some mince and chose to make apple crumble and custard for dessert. The secretary gave me an idea of how many I was to cook for so thought today we'll keep it simple.

When Mr Fischer, the headmaster, came in to introduce himself he was very nice, I liked him instantly. Sometime later Carol, my first lady, came in she was so lovely, and of course had to fill me in on how things were. I was shocked to hear I had two lunch clubs to send out meals to every Wednesday, that sounded scary. I had a lot to take in, lunch numbers were around eighty at this time, the lunch clubs were for fifty and twenty, this should be fun I thought and I was glad to have Carol for support. Two more ladies came in at different stages and this was our team. This kitchen was fairly nice and with a proper serving hatch, not like Germany but better than Astor School.

Gradually I got into the swing of it and I liked the fact no management were there making rules so I could make my own choices.

I came into work nearly two hours before my real starting time, as wasn't like Germany, I had all the potatoes to peel myself and all the vegetable preparation. Carol was a great help and helped me get settled in. It wasn't so long before I became so organised and liked to reach a certain stage before any of the ladies came in, first course and dessert in the oven, potatoes and veg pans ready to go on, custard steamer pot ready to make the custard, no long handled whisk this time as in Germany, of course Wednesdays were even more busy with the children and the two lunch clubs. I did like the fact that none of the management showed their faces and I could please myself. My area co-ordinator had spoken to me on the phone as there was plenty of paperwork to do and before long my first visit from the Environmental Health Officer, here it was Irene Lindsay. She was strict but really nice, we didn't really much care for these visits but that was part of cooking. The younger of my two ladies left and Debbie and Jackie joined us, this became a nice team that lasted over four years, all were nice ladies to work with and we shared some real fun adventures. Those first years were so nice, I could make pleasing choices that must have been working as our numbers had started to increase.

I had to attend meetings held in different schools, it let me get to know some of the other cooks and compare notes and ideas. Mr Fischer, our headmaster was good fun and came in each day for a chat, he liked a laugh and to teasingly torment Carol, he was also a 'sort of fun snob' and liked to hear about my work at Clarence House. Once I knew him more I brought in some of my memorabilia from those years to show him, he liked that. Many aspects of the catering company amused me such as during training. What training I would think, I was never given any, mind you I liked it that way.

I was able to make the kitchen my own domain and felt it got better and better, the rise in meat numbers and increase in both lunch club numbers confirmed this. I had my own standards and refused to use ready peeled potatoes as I felt that the quality was poor. I ordered as much more fresh fruit and veg as I dared and what they either stopped or wouldn't provide I brought in myself. There was so much paperwork, invoice books, ledgers of all sorts for my ordering. I was fine with that, getting to know all the company phone people, the dinner registers and money to sort out. I took much of the paperwork home and Tony came to my rescue, he was very neat and exact and much better at it than I was and we got ourselves into a nice routine, I think he quite enjoyed it most of the time except perhaps for monthly stock check. Every Friday I sat and wrote out all the cheques into their log book, often feeling so tired after work and during this tedious task that I'd find I'd dozed off and feel the pen slide across the page and wake me.

As well as this, to add interest in food and create higher numbers Tony used his talent in drawing to draw great menu drawings that became more elaborate over the years. The children loved to comment on them and the numbers were creeping up, I think this is why the company mostly left us alone and I liked it that way. We were a good team who worked hard with Carol, Jackie and Debbie. We had some great laughs and got to know each other very well, it was all working beautifully.

In summer the kitchen got too hot, I remember once Debbie saying 'you could grow bananas in here!'

We had some laughs with Mr Fischer too, one time he chose to eat with us in the kitchen as he sometimes did. Carol set him a very special place, a serving fork and spoon in his place and sugar dredger for salt, he liked the fun, or the time he said he would give me a car run to my meeting, when I went outside to see two big cards in his front window one saying 'Mike' the other 'Alice'. Not expected on a Mercedes! We laughed so much and he drove me there like that! He was a kind man with a great sense of humour; it was a pleasure knowing him.

Mr Fischer was having some teacher interviews and asked if I would do a buffet lunch, it was hard work in the midst of our meals. I did all the shopping, asking for the money needed and I did a great deal of the work at home, working until 1am if necessary and of course needed Tony's help for shopping and to carry in prepared food on the day, he was always happy to support me good naturedly. The girls and I enjoyed doing all the last bits during our work, of course this was nothing to do with the company, I just prayed no one would come in.

We were, of course, extra busy on these days but got great feedback, all so well received. I quite often was asked to do either small lunches for special guests of Mr Fischer or sometimes for a teacher with a guest. I always made these very special, not every day meals, it was good to have quite a few of these days and small functions, it gave me another skill not needed for everyday meals.

Chapter 20

Christmas

We were always very busy and soon it would be the festive season. I started to get all my ordering done and Tony had drawn spectacular menus both for the lunch clubs and for the children. The school lunch numbers went up for that day and the same with the lunch clubs. All was going to plan till the turkey meat was due to come in, sadly not fresh like in Germany – these were frozen. On the arrival of the meat, I was horrified to see they had sent pork, not turkey, as supply had been short. I was fuming, all the menus were prepared, I had tears of anger in my eyes. I thought I'm not having this so I phoned the company office to query this, their reply, just give them pork, I couldn't believe that and lost my cool, saying 'if you want to serve them pork you have to come in and cook it, I won't, I refuse!' I could hear her talk to someone in the background saying 'she's furious and refuses to accept this!' Soon Carol came in and I told her of this, they had ended the phone conversation saying 'leave it with me.' What a morning that was, the phone never stopped ringing, them saying 'we're doing our best.'

Mr Fischer arrived and I told him what had happened, he'd known me as a very calm person who now saw I could hold my own if needed and I wasn't going to back down and accept this. Carol was laughing as she told Debbie and Jackie of our plight and asked them if they had seen any men in striped suits outside Iceland! Eventually a caller said 'your turkeys will get there can you wait till they arrive and put in for overtime for yourself?' It was very funny when I got home and Tony came in and I told him 'I made all the managers jump today.' He made me laugh saying 'just wait till I go to the corner shop for a cigar and tell me how it all happened.'

So we were able to serve as good a standard meal as you can with frozen turkey, I was very proud to assure potatoes, veg and gravy were perfect and the day was enjoyed all round. Mr Fischer, the teachers and children all enjoyed Christmas dinner together. I didn't much like the fact that we, the kitchen team, had to weave our way through the tables with me carrying the Christmas pudding while the children sang 'We want figgy pudding' at the top of their voices.

It was quite embarrassing walking round.

Tony always created superb Christmas decorations at home, our home was never ordinary and he didn't like tacky or showy and never outdoors, just the usual enjoyable event of the day. We went for a long walk to collect our branches, always a wonderful family outing and so special, and we enjoyed our Christmas Day, loving being a family. Tony's Mum and Dad always spent Christmas Day with his sister Theresa and her family and they came to us on Boxing Day. A time or two we spent New Year's Day with Theresa and family and our boys and Great Nanny, Sheila's Mum. Theresa had two boys, Russell and Nicky, similar ages to Christopher and Stuart, and she now had two younger boys with Clive her second husband, Craig and Calvin. Sheila, Tony's Mum, loved her six grandsons and was very good to them all, she would have loved a granddaughter. We loved the times we could all spend together; Sheila and Les especially loved these times.

It was nice being back in the country as we were able to visit Betty, Brian and Gordon in Swindon and to make trips to Scotland to visit the rest of the family.

In the four years I worked with Jackie, Debbie and Carol we were a great team and had plenty of laughs and personal conversations. I was sad when Carol was thinking of leaving as she felt she would like to go into nursing. Before she left Mr Fischer was almost at retirement age and was going to leave so there would be big changes. We did a buffet for Mr Fischer and his wife. When the time came, I had a real think about what would be a suitable leaving gift from the kitchen team and came up with what I felt was the perfect idea. I got my friend Greta who worked in London to go to Fortnum and Mason to buy two tins of their special tea and chocs, it felt perfect as we boxed and wrapped these, he was delighted noting the high class shop they came from, just right for his nature.

A time later we had a thank you letter from Mr Fischer saying how he had enjoyed our gift even though he got told off from Mrs Fischer for putting tea leaves down the sink! He also said he had used his best Royal Doulton tea service – very Mr Fischer, nice letter with another little torment for Carol, over the past years they had loved to tease each other with humour the letter held another little torment for Carol once again.

A little time before he left I forgot the mention of a special dinner party for fourteen he had asked me to do as he was interviewing for a new head teacher for St Mary's. The day was a great success and everyone really enjoyed the special lunch though Mrs Waller, who got the job, told me later she was too nervous to eat that day, she seemed very nice as we were introduced.

Christopher and Stuart were now teenagers, each had their own small group of friends, and were enjoying life at Archers Court School. They both chose to walk to and from the school though it was a decent walk, Stuart still loved sport, especially football and was an avid supporter of Liverpool. Christopher was taking more interest in history and trying to work hard to gain good school marks, it wasn't easy for him, he really had to work to achieve his aims. In truth Stuart was the better scholar in many ways but I think lack of confidence was still an issue with him. He was good at Maths, English and Art in some ways. I was very proud when the school secretary said our two boys were the nicest lads in school, with their very good manners and behaviour, of course I loved that. At one of our parent evenings one of Christopher's teachers said 'he's had a little try at being a Jack the lad, but gave up as he couldn't carry it off, he's too well bred,' again appealed to me; of course our boys were well bred with immaculate manners, we were very proud of them. Stuart too always had favourable comments on parent teacher days. It was hard to believe how fast they were growing up.

Tony started work with Group Four, his first job after the army. This wasn't the job he had wanted, he did have an interview for the type of work he wanted but was unlucky then, after a few months they called him back and he got the job. This was at a young offenders institution at Dover's Western Heights and he quickly settled into life there, his place of work was on a historic site and of course this was of very great interest to Christopher who was keen to gain as much knowledge as possible as to the history of it all.

Now Tony was well settled in this new work since a few months after I had started at the school.

Carol was now ready to leave, I was sorry to lose her though I still had Debbie and Jackie, but in Carol's place we had a few changes of lady.

We were asked if we would take a NVQ course in Nutritional health and agreed to this and spent some days after work sitting to do some of the paperwork. In a way it was quite good fun though kept us very busy for two or three months and we had a verifier come in to assess our work. Debbie was very good at this, her work was very detailed and accurate; we all managed to pass the course. Before we got our certificates there was some problem at the college I had to keep on at them to insist we got our certificates, which took some time and effort on my part, we'd done the work and passed so deserved this and I made sure we got it.

All this work added to our interest in the healthy eating programme, Debbie was very artistic and made and had laminated an impressive poster for our kitchen. Tony's menus too added to the healthy eating scheme, it was all good to be seen by anyone who came in to our kitchen especially the E. H. Officers. Our meal numbers were still increasing we were now serving at least one hundred meals a day from the eighty or so at first, the Wednesday Senior Citizens lunch club numbers had increased too, from fifty to seventy and the smaller club from twenty to twenty five.

This was all good in helping the management team to leave us alone.

Since we had made our home in Dover we enjoyed having family visits now and then, Meg lived nearest, she was still in Epsom; Celia was now grown up and James and Shereen were similar ages to our boys, Betty and Brian visited from Swindon, and Gordon was now an adult. It was always nice to have any of them, at another time Chris and Eric came to stay also Bill, Jackie and their youngest son Neil, it was a great pleasure to have them and show them round Dover. All our children were growing up fast.

When Stuart's sixteenth birthday was near I planned to take him on a surprise visit to Liverpool Stadium, he was a devoted fan, included was a tour round followed by lunch in the Directors' Box. This worked out well as we were having a new kitchen fitted at home, Christopher and Tony would oversee the work.

We travelled to London Victoria station for our overnight coach and = we were there in plenty of time. What hadn't been made clear when I had booked was that we had to take the Blackpool coach and we actually watched that pull out! Of course I felt very foolish, I did feel the booking office should have made that clear.

Now I had to try to make other plans and this late at night it wasn't easy.

So there we were stranded in London. I did phone the train station, the last one had gone and no more coaches that night, oh help! We tried to contact Greta, with no luck, it was at least a warm dry night and the two of us spent the night in St. James Park right opposite Clarence House my old home! We shouldn't have been in there really as closed at night but it was fine, nice and quiet, poor Stuart was very tired. I was sorry to have made such an error and would later complain to the company not making me aware if this. The next morning we got the fast train to Liverpool! There could still have been one or two people I knew at Clarence House or Marlborough House Mews, but it too late at night to try that so we just made do. I never phoned Tony till we were safely there and had been to our boarding house that we had booked and in plenty of time for our booked day out at the stadium. Of course Tony and Christopher found the whole thing hilarious when I told them, as did Debbie at work, she thought it was very funny and never forgot it. I can assure you neither did Stuart and I but it was all part of life's adventure!

There was to be more staff changes in my kitchen as both Debbie and Jackie had heard of a new warehouse shop opening in Dover and had both passed an interview and would leave on the same day, though I didn't blame them as their wages were poor, but I knew I'd miss the happy team we had become and worried to as to how I would cope.

It was never hard to find people who wanted school time work and Jackie and Debbie knew two ladies to fill their jobs, it's quite hard having two change at once but we would get there. My two new ladies were Lesley and Lyn, we had one more place to fill as my third lady had changed a few times, eventually we were joined by Jo and she was quite a character, as we were to learn. Lyn did wonder if she would take to the job, because at first she wasn't that sure, they had to work hard and I made more work than many schools who were quite hurried and uncaring about their work. The very comparison in school meal numbers assured me this was true, we had high numbers and served good meals as much as possible and set out the tables and benches each day as we had a shared hall that had to become the dining hall.

After a short time Lyn relaxed and liked the job, she and Lesley settled in well and Lyn found Jo's company great fun, she really was a unique character, we saw that from the start. Jo was a great worker and was very strong and liked us to know that, with all her stories of various jobs ranging from work on a farm to pub work she had many past jobs and never left us short of a laugh. Lyn found her antics a delight, as we all did, her stories of how she pre-made all of her Christmas lunch so that she could just enjoy the day and have her husband and son both dress up, even in bow ties, for lunch, they also had a daughter, her stories were very funny. We also noted with concern how she drank so much coke, to almost addiction level, we were sure that wasn't good for her. Chris came to join our team, I think for a time Chris and Jo were both there, we had some special lunches for book week and we all dressed up for an Alice in Wonderland theme. Tony drew some excellent pictures for the menu, we managed to get a Jumbo teapot and items to set the table behind the serving hatch so the children could see it while being served – they loved it, we had a lot of fun.

We always had plenty of small buffets that I was asked to do, the girls loved helping with these, most I did at home the night before though there was still plenty to set up the next day.

I was flattered to overhear Jo say to someone 'you don't need any crisps at any buffet Alice does,' thank you Jo I liked that.

As she was an army wife Jo came in one day to tell us that her husband was being posted to another regiment and they would be moving to near Salisbury. Jo was good fun and a hard worker, we would miss her. On her last week she handed in her uniform and she came in while the girls were setting up the dining room on her last day, as she went in there I could hear much laughter, Jo had worn her own choice of uniform, this being a scarf tied in turban style to cover her hair and looking old fashioned overall. Lyn was laughing so much she came into the kitchen almost falling with laughter at Jo's choice of uniform, Lyn thinking she looked like Peggy from the comedy T.V. series Hi-de-Hi. I was laughing at Lyn! It was a precious memorable moment.

With Lesley, Lyn and Chris we really settled in to become a happy team of friends over the next seven years, Loose Women had nothing on our chats and personal stories. Mrs Waller, our Headmistress, did make comment on what a good, happy team we were.

It was good to enjoy the nice long summer break from work.

One year we had a family wedding in Scotland so we chose to book a caravan for two weeks, it was really nice to have invitations to Chris and Eric, John and Margaret as well as Bill and Jackie and as always to visit Bunty, Mary and Willie.

The wedding was of Chris's daughter Marianne, she was a beautiful bride and her partner John so handsome in his McDonald tartan kilt. It was a lovely day and to feel that love and warmth when so many of our family could be together, these times were and are always special for us. John's wife Margaret, who suffers some health issues and chooses not to attend many functions, says she feels that she will attend any functions with the Young's because of the great atmosphere created. She pays us a great compliment in saying 'oh no you'd never get any jealousy between any of the Young's, it wouldn't happen' thank you Margaret you too are a delightful part of our family, we love you so much, as we do with Jackie, Bill's wife.

Marianne had the loveliest wedding cake I had ever seen, it was spectacular. It was done to represent the church with pink icing made to look like a red carpet going up the tiers to look like steps. Her wedding day was wonderful and Chris as mother of the bride, looked wonderful.

We enjoyed our time in the caravan, making me think back to some other holidays we enjoyed as a family.

Before we went to Germany for the second time we bought a large family tent, it was very exciting for us, it had three bedrooms, we used two and a wardrobe room, a living area and kitchen recess. To try it the first time we had a most enjoyable holiday in the New Forest, which sadly was the time of the Marchioness boat disaster. The next time was a holiday in Bavaria, it was fabulous, the boys were a little older by this time and could help put up the tent. As I think back to that first time when I saw all the poles Tony had tipped out I had visions of us using the canvas as a ground sheet to sleep on, it looked so complicated! Of course Tony was used to tents and was so organised that he colour coded all the poles that first time to make it easier.

We used the tent again in Germany, this time near to the Denmark border, the place was called Damp and it sure was very much so. While near there looking round one day I was so astonished to almost bump into a lady who was cashier in our local shop when we were so far from our area in Sennelager, we greeted each other, our German was little and she was the same with English. When we met in the supermarket on our return she was telling her manager.

It was as we drove back from that holiday, a day early because of the wet, that we heard on the car radio that President Gorbachev was overthrown.

With us living back home now and, for the first time, nearer to Tony's Mum and Dad, and now able to visit them lots or them to come to us as Sheila didn't much like us being away. It was now in these years she and I became great friends, we had always got on very well but we were either in Windsor or Germany so we had so little time together. It was nice too being nearer Theresa and Clive and our boys' four cousins Russell, Nick, Craig and Calvin, Tony's sister and family.

We did enjoy one holiday with Sheila and Les, we booked a caravan in Scotland in a glorious setting by The Dornoch Firth, the scenery I loved very much indeed as it was on part of our journey to and from The Castle of Mey.

At other times Les booked family outings for us to enjoy lavish buffets on board The Smorgasbord, we loved those outings with Tony's family, Les loved having his daughter and son's families together, as did Sheila.

Ahead of each new term we had two cleaning days, it was always nice to see Chris, Lesley and Lyn after the break and to catch up with all our news. These were more relaxed days with no lunches to prepare. Between work we had extra cups of tea and could relax. One year they chose to put in new fans and we came in to real mayhem; the work wasn't completed so it was hard to get the kitchen cleaned up and ready, there was dust and debris everywhere, we had to work very hard. This new fan system was supposed to be a benefit, however we found this was not so in our first term back, it was a nightmare. For the gas for the ovens to work the fans had to be on, we found this made the kitchen freezing cold. We most certainly had some laughs over it especially when Lyn came in one day wearing long stripy socks and Chris with a hat over her ears, it was really unpleasant, any teacher who walked through commented on the cold chill, and it was very difficult to keep food hot during service. Of course I complained, telling them of the temperature in the kitchen, eventually they admitted that to cut cost they had left out an expensive part that would have eliminated this and now needed to be redone, in spite of our blue noses we had a lot of laughs because of it.

There was always some nightmare or other; the catering companies changed every few years, causing more mayhem even though I had to attend lots of meetings to hear how it was all to smoothly change over, that was a joke! It was havoc closing for one company, all stock had to go for new ones to set up. This time our new company said we're not to worry as all the orders were being placed and sent in, we just had to be there to take delivery, of course they never visited any kitchens to check storage etc. This turned out to be a massive mistake, it was just so ridiculous that it was hilarious, they so massively over ordered. We packed in all the dry goods we could, then the frozen food was delivered and 'wow' the amount was staggering, at that time I only had a chest freezer, it was very hard work. I had known Martin the Brakes firm driver for years, he was so good natured, but lost his cool as I refused to accept what we couldn't store and wouldn't sign for it. He had to take most of it back and understandably was none too pleased as we were not the first school to do so. However, he knew it wasn't our fault.

It took the girls and I ages to sort out just what we would use in the next two weeks, we couldn't accept more. We heard of one enterprising cook who managed to talk her local supermarket into holding some where some of the less intelligent accepted and wasted the food, it was a nightmare and yet not their fault, the company started on a very big loss. The ordering needed to be done by the cook in charge who knew the numbers, holding and storage. They learned a lesson after that fiasco.

Another changeover left us with no deliveries for a week at the start of term, I ended up buying bread, flour, margarine, cheese and milk to get us by.

Over all the years we had gained The White Cliffs Food Award that changed to two yearly and became Clean Food First Award.

As we were such a good team our standards just got better and better. We were very proud to serve the best quality food we could and this was much before the Jamie Oliver involvement. Our kitchen was to gain its own awards as I had a phone call one day to ask if I would consider to enter for The Heartbeat Award Scheme and agreed to this though I did feel very nervous as a Doctor of Nutrition would come in and oversee our work.

At least it was on a fixed date, though I was very nervous. The day came and Dr Jenny Paulton arrived and introduced herself, she was just so lovely and by the end of the day she made me feel like a million dollars! She was so very impressed with our work and our food standards and she just loved Tony's menu drawings and said our food was of the highest standard she'd seen, it was nice that she let Mrs Waller know of her findings and nice that she, in turn, put it on the newsletter for the parents to see. This gave us a great boost as we really did work very hard every single day; I was over the moon as I walked home that day. Dr Paulton had taken photocopies of our menus saying she had no hesitation in putting our school forward for the award. It was a real pat on the back for us.

Some weeks later I had to go to receive the certificate. Tony came with me and it was a really special evening out. The company never even said thank you to our team even though our meal numbers had increased and were really high. I know I that I created a lot of work for the girls to reach our own standards, but I was very proud of my team and wished that the company were more gracious and let us know of our value especially for my ladies who worked so hard. There was a time when we were taking in over £1,000 a week; I did all the banking on Saturdays.

Wednesdays and Fridays became hectic with most of the school children on lunches, we were exhausted but exhilarated by the time we went home. When finished we were pleased to sit and chat over a cup of tea, on Fridays we started to stop at a coffee house on the way home, that became our treat.

It really felt like I worked every day for the company as in the evenings Tony and I added the meal registers and set any money paid in ready to add to the weekly total. Tony's input was invaluable as he was much better than I was with the paperwork, we were even congratulated on neatest and most accurate bookwork and I know this was thanks to Tony. I always told the management that Tony did much of this for me, my flair was the cooking and ordering.

We had our kitchen running like clockwork, I made all my own quiche and pizzas and pitta breads, which became very popular. I refused to use their readymade items and introduced a spaghetti vegetable bake on Fridays which the children loved, never a bit left over.

Chapter 21

Family Life

Christopher and Stuart were now in their last years at school, both had a small group of special friends.

The time came for Christopher's two weeks of work experience; the first week he worked at Dover Harbour Board and he enjoyed this very much, his second week was at The Dover Museum and from then on he was 'hooked' as for the rest of the time he was in Dover he went to work there every Saturday on a voluntary basis.

Preparing for his exams he had to work very hard to achieve his aims, it wasn't easy for him but he did have enthusiasm in abundance for everything he undertook. He was very well respected as a pupil and chosen as a prefect and his name was put forward as the school's Head Boy. He didn't get this honour but one of the teachers did say that the wrong boy was picked as Head Boy.

Christopher took his responsibilities very seriously, becoming involved in anything that was going on at the school, Tony and I were very proud of him.

Stuart worked hard at school and did well in Maths, English and Art, though his real love was sport of all kinds. He had a small group of close friends and was well respected in their group and for a short time he was in a school football team and loved that, his Dad and I were always very proud of him for his immaculate good behaviour and manners.

Stuart is a quiet young man who suffered some lack of confidence, I was sorry to feel that I had given him this legacy, though his time in Germany was when I did see him grow in confidence; I loved that time for him.

His friends were Matt, Mark and Chris as well as some other lads who liked sport. Stuart gave us every reason to feel proud of him at parent teacher meetings, he had another year till his work experience and this was to work in a bank for one week and his second week in the school office. I think they were short of placements, though I loved it for him as for a second time the school secretary said to me what a delightful young man he was. I, of course, knew that already but loved to hear it again.

Whatever his choices were to be I knew Stuart would be dedicated and work hard.

Another school holiday almost at an end and Lesley, Lyn, Chris and I were on our cleaning days again. The place was in 'uproar' as some work had been done to remove asbestos so we had much cleaning up to do. As always the term was very busy and our meal numbers were very high. It was on a Wednesday, the day of our send out meals, that I got a phone call from the management to say that Mr Walker, who was the very head of the company, was going to come in and visit that day. 'Oh help' I thought as I went to tell the girls. As it turned out he was very nice indeed and thanked us for our hard work. I showed him some of our menu pictures which I kept in my office, he was very impressed and said that they were better than their own efforts. So this felt like a nice pat on the back for us as we truly felt at most times our hard work was never appreciated so it was very nice indeed.

There were always people coming into the kitchen, sometimes the EHO, Environmental Health Officer. We always cringed to see her and, though she was strict, Irene was very fair and we always got good pass marks. It made us nervous as she stood at the side and observed us serve up lunches.

There was also our area coordinator, over the years I had nice ones and ones I positively did not like.

A day of particular dislike was when Fred(rika) came in at the same time as another EHO, they were not my favourites by any means. Fred, as she liked to be known, my coordinator called in now and then and on this particular day my less popular EHO, Joanne, came as well. I felt the two of them were just so rude they actually stood behind us as we served up and I was aware of them whispering behind our backs, not like Irene who stood aside and simply observed as was her job to do. I was very cross, we were a hard working team in at least the top three for high meal numbers, if not first, so their rudeness was due to their lack of manners.

There was a competition for the kitchen with highest numbers and the prize was money and restaurant meal vouchers. I was so sure we would win this and I so looked forward to giving this treat to my ladies for all their hard work, I always believe Fred and her team kept this accolade for themselves as we never did hear who won it, I had my suspicion, however I had no proof.

Our standards continued to be high, every now and then we had buffets to do for one thing or another, these were not for the company, they were always private for the school, over the years I did so many of them.

Mrs Waller, our head teacher, came to me one day to say that there was to be a head teachers' conference held in our school on a non-pupils day and asked if I would do a buffet lunch, this was to be for one hundred and twenty or so. That day as there was no school Lesley, Lyn and Chris wouldn't be in so it was just me, but I agreed to do this. Mrs Waller gave me the money and Tony and I did all the shopping, I always had plenty of lists for these events. The day was hectic of course. I did much of the preparation at home, up most of the night doing so, however I was delighted to know it was a spectacular success. Mrs Waller was very pleased, I was a bit nervous when she came in afterwards taking me into the hall for them to say thank you. I was very proud really, one of the head teachers said that nowhere had they ever been had there been such a great selection, especially in the vegetarian section. It was very hard work but I have to say I loved the accolade. Many of them had personally come into the kitchen to say thank you as well. As always Tony's input was of great value making beautiful little food name labels as well as shopping and delivery of food to the school.

Chapter 22

Rob Roy MacGregor

Something was to trigger a memory that, although I had always known it, had stayed at the back of my mind, regarding my family history and this was to know we were descendants of the infamous Rob Roy MacGregor – an outlaw, I know, but was unjustified and should never have been so. Our own father was fiercely proud of his name, Colin MacGregor Young, given in his honour and we do know that Rob Roy was a man of great strength and honour to his own beliefs and as Chief of his Clan was held in much respect. I for one feel a great honour and pride in our ancestor, I know his word and his bond was strong and true. This in spite of the fact that Tony tells me in jest that we are from a family of bandits!

I am only sorry that this had not come to my thoughts at the time I had visited my Dad as I know he would have been proud to tell me of this, it would have been a great conversation. Sadly I saw him so few times and now of course it's too late.

Our next time in Scotland was at the invitation of Jackie, my brother Bill's wife, as she wanted Betty and I to be surprise guests at a party she had secretly planned for Bill's fiftieth birthday. It was a great event and so lovely to be with so many of my family again and to see their children all so grown up now.

On many of our visits to Scotland Tony and I stayed with Chris and Eric, we loved being with them and Chris and I would sit up chatting till the early hours of morning. Betty and Brian always had a home in Scotland with Brian's sister Freda while Meg, Paul and family stayed with Bunty on visits and also had Sandy and Jean who lived nearby for extra beds.

At any time alone with my sisters there was always some sharing of memories or chats on our thoughts of each of our individual lives and our ideas of how our childhood years had been, I'm sure my brothers had the same thoughts too, I know Bill did as he and I were so close for some years. Or just when alone with one sister to chat over their feelings as none of us truly understood why our lives had turned out as they did, it's almost like a question that is always there.

Again at the school I had another phone call to ask if I would enter to gain another 'Heartbeat Award' for healthy eating and a date was set for a day of observation, we were really very pleased as we felt we had increased our healthy eating in our kitchen as I made home-made soups, bread and still the now popular filled pitta breads. We felt our kitchen was running very smoothly as indeed did our second Dr of Nutrition, she loved how we served our fruit and salads. She too was very impressed and had no hesitation in saying we would receive the award and I would be notified of the ceremony. For this event it was held at the Friary at Aylesford and was a day time event. I left the girls to do the lunch, they enjoyed the challenge.

At the Friary the event was being broadcast on live radio from the venue, it was very enjoyable, we were served, of course, a very health conscious buffet before the ceremony of handing out certificates. On receiving the programme I was very surprised to note I was to receive a second award as I had been put forward for a 'Commitment to Excellence Award'. Of course I was very thrilled at this though once more I later noted there was no thank you from the company, yet they used word of these awards when it suited them. Still, I loved to win it just for our team; Chris, Lyn, Lesley and I worked very hard in our kitchen. We had lots of laughs too and plenty of fun conversations; remember the pelvic floor exercise talks Lyn? Or if there was something interesting, basically gossip, I'd say to Lyn 'I've got something to tell you when you've changed and come into the kitchen,' she loved that and hurried to get into uniform, we had so many of these fun moments. Or I'd say to Leslie, who was first in, that I'd tell her when Lyn and Chris were in. Lyn was always eager to hurry and hear whatever the incident worth repeating was, lovely moments, great girls, I loved working with them. We did have some stand in ladies sometimes when Lesley was off with a bad back for a spell and when Chris came in saying she had been offered to go on a holiday with her husband Phil, we said of course she must go.

Christopher and Stuart were very busy revising for exams, our house always seemed to have lots of art projects going on, this year was very important for Christopher as he was now doing his A level exams.

Life was always very busy both at home and at school, both our boys continued to enjoy school and time with their friends, Christopher was always very involved with school events, such as a dinner which they had to serve to the teachers and he still spent his Saturdays at the museum in Dover. He and two other friends took a great interest in Dover's Western Heights and loved learning of the history of it all so much that they began to form a plan to become involved in many presentation projects and this led them to become founder members of the Western Heights Preservation Society. It had very small beginnings but did not remain so.

Sometimes on Sundays Christopher and his Dad enjoyed long walks together, Stuart wasn't so much into that, though it was always together as a family that we enjoyed going out for a walk to find our branch for our Christmas tree when the time came. That was always a great pleasure and one of my fondest memories as something we enjoyed doing every year.

Christmas at St Mary's School was always a very busy time, nowhere more so than in the kitchen.

Mrs Waller had made some changes in that the staff Christmas lunch was on a different day to the children. There was so much planning that had to be done to make sure I had all that I needed to be as I wanted it, never forgetting the Christmas they wanted me to serve pork. Now I carefully ordered as much as I could in advance, as you never knew what cost cutting ideas the company would come up with, such as not allowing us to wrap the chipolatas in bacon. They wanted to use the ready peeled potatoes and frozen vegetables, but not for me – I used fresh. Remember the carrots girls? I'm sure you do, as we had two Christmas dinner days, on the afternoon before each, after we had finished our normal day's lunches, we made a pot of tea and sat on stools round our steel table, each with chopping boards, and filled an enormous pot with the carrots we sat to prepare carrot batons as that's how I liked them done. It was an enormous task; we enjoyed plenty of chat and laughter and some funny shapes too! While at this task we opened the tin of sweets Mrs Waller gave us to share for Christmas or had a freshly made mince pie. This was another product they stopped us using, I didn't mind for the children as most didn't like them, but how could I stop making them for the senior citizens when I had first-hand seen how much they enjoyed them? I noted many wrap them and take them home for their tea. The staff enjoyed them too so even if it meant I had to buy the mincemeat I always made around 130 of them, senior citizens were the send out Wednesday lunches and the mince pies were much enjoyed after Christmas lunch each year, they liked me to walk down to the church hall so that they could say thank you. I told my Clarence House friend Terry that I felt like the Queen as I had to go round the tables chatting to them, Terry and I laughed over that!

As well as the carrots that day I prepared all the potatoes. As our numbers were very high it really was the most enormous task as on the children's day it was Christmas lunch for around two hundred and eighty and the next day (or one before) was normal lunch for 130 children plus Christmas lunch for seventy five senior lunch club and a second Christmas lunch for perhaps twenty five staff (teachers); it took some sorting out. I can still picture the two pots of freshly prepared carrots batons where most cooks would have taken the easier option and cut them in rounds and with two enormous pots of potatoes prepared and ready, yes we worked very hard indeed. On the actual days every oven was filled with potatoes roasting in big trays, and all the sausages, meat and stuffing. Being cooked were enormous pots of gravy and brandy sauce (adult day). I had the mince pies already made as well as the Xmas puddings, now in the steamer, the task was a marathon and it was four o'clock at least before we finished. We took great pride in serving Christmas lunches that were very hot, very fresh and of the highest standard that was possible with their restrictions. Lesley, Lyn and Chris had every reason to feel proud of how much work they had done. After having done two days of nearing three hundred meals we set the table for our own Christmas lunch, it was always 4pm before we were to eat. The dining room staff joined us for this, Jenny, Barbara, Janice and Janet, the longer term ladies I can think of, we had some great laughs, some less long term ladies had joined us one year. We always put one present in to raffle. To see the picture of Lyn's face when she got the smallest parcel, she was very excited, eagerly opened it to find a somewhat strange object, we never did decide what exactly it was. Of course it had set her, then us, off with tears of laughter yet trying to be polite and not laugh as of course someone had bought it. That was always a very exhausting week though nice to feel we had done it so well.

Tony's drawings for Christmas week were always very special and his Christmas menus were spectacular; the senior lunch club loved the special menus made for them. I had a great relationship with Mr and Mrs Blair who ran the lunch club and they loved the menus provided. I made some very nice friends through the lunch club.

Christopher completed his exams and gained the marks he needed to go to university. At first he didn't get his number one choice, then I got a call to say a place was available at his first choice of Goldsmiths University in London. He had taken part time work at a DIY store and I rushed down to tell him as had to accept by a certain time, so he was very pleased and this was soon to be the start of a new life for him. I so loved his last school report where each teacher wrote their own findings after the marks, that report would have made any mother proud where they said 'Christopher is a very likeable young man whose work just gets better and better' every page had a complimentary write up and of course we were indeed very proud of him.

Stuart too had very nice reports, one which said that he had a very good attitude to school. He was going to continue for an extra year at school on an IT course, he was never so certain of any career choices he wanted to fulfil.

Soon it was the time for Christopher to go to university. I hated not to have him at home with us and of course worried constantly about him, though it really pleased me that if I wanted to I could get on a coach right to the gates of Goldsmiths from our home in Dover. As it was, Christopher phoned us every day full of joy and enthusiasm at every stage of what he was doing, working, sightseeing or walking in Greenwich Park seeing the squirrels, he settled in and was very happy.

He enjoyed coming home and having nights out with his friends Dean, Dan and Ben as well as to enjoy all the new friends he had made in London. He was so thoughtful, looking out for some of the girls meeting them off the train when late, though I worried for his safety too, well I am a Mum!

It was in his second year at University when he phoned to say he wanted to bring his girlfriend home to meet up, over that weekend Tamsyn was introduced to us. Stuart was enjoying life with a nice group of friends; I liked the way they all looked out for each other. One friend must have worked in a Post Office club as they all became members and went there regularly, he was having lots of fun, they did all sorts over the next year or so, went to bowling, the cinema, ice skating, many different pursuits. When he left school Stuart just wanted to work and for a time was very busy with agency work, he worked very hard, he was never idle or out of work and saved his money very well. He started to have driving lessons. A father of his friend saw that he was a good reliable worker and was able to get him an interview with a major food supermarket, he got that job and settled happily to his working life – my boys really were growing up.

Stuart continued his love of sport and was able to enjoy going to top sport events such as the golf at Sandwich and cricket at Canterbury, it gave him a chance to enjoy those free days, he also went to Liverpool one time to see his team play and no Mum with him this time to watch our bus go.

I was now getting ready for Sandra's visit, the date was all set, it was just before school holiday and a fairly busy time as there were two buffets I was asked to do on a Friday and following Monday. The Friday buffet was small but the one on Monday was much bigger and I was relieved when they were over.

Christopher was going to meet Sandra at the airport and bring her home to Dover. By that time I finished work and would be ready to welcome her. It was a long flight for her on her own and she was no doubt feeling very apprehensive, having not seen each other for so many years. Her husband John and daughter Sonja had flights some days earlier as they had some visits up North to make, then they would then join Sandra here in Dover in the next few days.

It was just so wonderful to welcome her at our home and made the years seem to roll away, sadly we weren't young again! It was nice for us to meet each other's family as we had always kept in touch. These days were a great highlight in my life. Ahead of John and Sonja's arrival, Christopher loved taking Sandra on a tour of Canterbury Cathedral and to Dover Castle, he was very knowledgeable on the history of both places and loved showing her round. I made sure I was home from work as early as possible during their visit. The day came for John and Sonja to join us. That morning Tony was off duty and had taken Sandra on a long walk up Langdon Cliff in Dover and I managed to squeeze in time to prepare a buffet for us at home. Though John and Sonja were going on to one of his relatives, I managed to talk him into asking his cousin if it could be the next day so that we could relax, party and get to know each other with both Stuart and Christopher with us. It was such a happy day where we were able to relax and have what was a very special get together. Their visit had been such a delight, we loved having them and it was so nice to meet John and Sonja and during those days Sandra visited my school kitchen to be able to know where I worked. When making up a bed for Sonja I had bought a tiny teddy bear for her to put in her bed and Tony had made a miniature passport for it photo and all! A fun gift for her to keep. I was sad to see them go off on the next stage of their tour, this was to Norway to visit relatives of Sandra's side of the family.

It was always nice to have Tony's Mum and Dad for visits, though Sheila felt all was not right with Les and we were sad to learn tests were able to confirm he had Parkinson's Disease. Some time before this we had so enjoyed a family party that Clive had planned for Theresa, Tony's sister, for her fortieth birthday. I think Theresa and I did the buffet, it was a most enjoyable evening with many relatives there, though at the very end as we were leaving Les had a bad fall in the car park. It was very alarming though he refused to have a hospital check and was left with plenty of aches and bruises.

As Tony worked every second weekend, visiting wasn't always easy though I did say to Tony that we must visit more and support your Mum with your Dad's illness. Sheila and I talked every day on the phone, my mother in law and I were really very good friends.

On that party night Christopher managed to take some photos that were very special, which Sheila loved, he took a lovely family photo especially for her of Tony and Theresa with their Mum and Dad. That night we also managed to get their six grandsons together for a lovely photo, Sheila had always wanted a nice photo of them all together.

There was lots of excitement in the build-up to the Millennium, the school held a party in the playground and the parent teacher group did most of the food and we made some additions, everyone had lots of fun. Again this was our busy season with the Christmas lunches to prepare once more in our usual way. This time some groups of children were going to come in and make some biscuits, these would be nicely packed for them to deliver to the elderly while they sang them some Christmas carols. A local newspaper photographer came in to take a photo of the children making them.

Some years back along with the staff in the dining hall we booked a Christmas night out for a meal sometimes at a club where there was a dance after. Lyn loved that, she loved to have a dance; we always enjoyed the evening out together over the years at quite a few different venues.

This was a busy year at home too as we had big plans for our own family celebration to mark this new century.

Terry and I always talked on the phone together and he wanted to invite Tony and I to have a Christmas meal with him in London, as we had done since our return from Germany.

Chapter 23

The Family Cairn

This was a very special New Year ahead to celebrate a new century and we most certainly intended to do that.

Tony was creating some very special artistic decoration for our house. As his plan came together I loved his choice, he had chosen a dark coloured paper to represent the night sky, in one corner he designed the 1999 zooming downwards, in the top corner year 2000 zooming in adding moon and stars, it looked very effective, Tony really was very good at this.

For my part I had an idea that I wanted to create a family cairn each with a family first and last name initial. We chose granite stones and I ordered the 21 initials to be made in a shoe repair shop as they did house names etcetera, the man liked my idea. They had to be weather proof so these were expensive but it was all coming together, however I did need Tony to plan how we could make this work in the centre of our front garden. It would have a water fountain to run over the stones; I embroidered a plain flag with the Taft family Cairn on it.

I also wrote a poem to explain the reason for our cairn, this would be launched at midnight by pouring champagne over it and with the flag on top; this was our own unique family celebration.

The Family Cairn

A pile of stones is what we've got
It doesn't sound an awful lot
Till you explain the reason why.
The reason is like this you see
A stone for you, a stone for me
Initialled each will tell a tale
Each stone is blessed with love and strength

Of memories both old and new
This cairn of love will represent
Togetherness in each event
We will help each other through
When times are good and sometimes bad
When we're happy and when we're sad
Like this cairn we've put together
We can master any weather
The millennium is here at last
Together we can face life's tasks
So year 2000 come on in
Embrace our lives and help us win

These 21 stones each with a family initial to represent the 21st century – it felt very special. Christopher and Stuart as well as Sheila and Les and Tamsyn were with us, it was the very best way to bring in this special year to share this celebration, it is just a pity all twenty one of us couldn't have been together though I made sure we took some photos and had copies of the poem.

Christopher turned 21 years old and I went to Goldsmiths to take him out and give him his gift. Tamsyn had an exam that afternoon and couldn't join us.

When I got home Stuart said 'I've passed my driving test,' I didn't believe him as he'd never said that he had a date for the test, so I thought it was his mock until he repeated, 'I passed my driving test.' I was very pleased for him and now he was keen to get a car, so I'll always remember that it was on Christopher's 21st birthday. Soon after he asked his Dad to come and look at a car he had seen, it was a nice red Corsa, of course now I worried about him driving – Mums!

Christopher completed his BA and planned to take his MA, gaining a place at Leicester University for this. Tamsyn gained her degree and was ready for a career in teaching.

Tony and I very much looked forward to the day of his graduation. When the time came for that it was so lovely, we were very proud. As we were in London, Meg said she and Paul would like to join us, it was really nice and we all went out for a meal afterwards.

Stuart was still enjoying life and all his activities, having his car gave him a new freedom.

Christopher and Tamsyn became engaged, though they were to wait for some time before they would be married.

The next summer Tony and I planned a trip to Scotland, our first holiday without our boys, though it did mean that we wouldn't be with Stuart for his 21st birthday, but he didn't mind as he was working. Tony and I bought him a set of golf clubs as he still loved all his sport.

We drove to Scotland and enjoyed visits to the family. After visiting Bunty we went on to see Mary and Willie, they had bought a lovely new flat with a warden. Willie was quite frail now and I felt concern when Mary said she was having stomach trouble.

On our way back Tony and I planned to make a special detour to Callander as I was very eager to visit the grave of our ancestor Rob Roy MacGregor. As we arrived late in the day we chose to book into a hotel for the night, and to have a look round Callander and the Rob Roy Centre there and visit the grave the next day.

The next morning we enjoyed a drive through The Trossach Trail. Loch Katrine was simply stunning, to see the shadow of the trees shimmering on the water, it was a perfect day and I was enthralled. We drove on to Balquhidder, again the scenery was magnificent. As we stood by the family grave it was with tears in my eyes that I felt the strength of pride on reading the headstone with the inscription saying 'MacGregor Despite Them.'

I know that I would love to stand on that same spot one day with Christopher and Stuart. Meg, Betty and Chris too would also have felt the emotion standing there, who knows, perhaps one day.

Once back at work, with Christopher settled in for his year in Leicester, Tony and I were going to have a weekend there to visit him. He was in a very high rise flat for his hall of residence; it had a great view over the city.

Tamsyn had started a teaching post and travelled to visit Christopher every second weekend or so, they enjoyed exploring the area together.

Again we were back at work and as always the days were busy with all the usual ups and downs. As always, Chris, Lyn, Lesley and I enjoyed great conversations and some good laughs, Lyn still loved it when there was some interesting bit of gossip and she would rush to get into her uniform to hear whatever it was.

We still of course had visits from Fred and either Irene or Joanne EHO (officer), and as always, I preferred Irene.

The big thermal metal food containers for the send out senior citizens lunches were always packed up by Leslie and I before a van came to collect them for the short drive to St Mary's Church Hall. This made Wednesdays so hectic, as well as because many of the children liked to come in for Wednesday roast lunch as well as Friday chip day, these were our most hectic days.

I had a variety of menus for the lunch club, they loved cottage pie, chicken pie or casserole, and I had plenty of very nice feedback over their desserts, they loved the sponges with fruit on the bottom, apricot being their firm favourite. All the desserts were very popular. Of course having different menus to the children made the work harder the pots being heavier or more of them left me with what I called my 'Wednesday arm', as it always ached more than usual after the heavy days work. Leslie too felt the strain, as my first lady in we were the two who packed the thermal boxes for the send out lunch. Lesley, Lyn and Chris had all the hard work of the tables and benches each day before and after lunch as well as the marathon amount of washing up to be done. Lesley did have some time off with back pain, and we had a stand in lady to fill these times, this was Dawn, who we got to know quite well. She was quite a character, she had three daughters of her own, all clever and doing well at school. Dawn's own life was another matter. She had met and planned to marry, so we had all her wedding news. We did have lots of reservations of her choice and tried to make her think it though, but there was no changing her mind and we were all invited to her wedding in the local registry office. That was quite an event, Dawn looked pretty, then her future husband walked in, it was very funny, he was dressed exactly like in the film The Great Gatsby, it was difficult to be serious especially when the time came for him to kiss the bride! We thought he was never going to release her, it was embarrassing. The reception was light hearted and fun. We felt something wasn't right, and were sorry when the marriage only lasted a month. We think he was already married though never knew all the facts, but we had told Dawn of our suspicion.

Stuart had saved a deposit to enable him to have his own place and chose a flat that was very near to our house. He enjoyed getting it all in order and moving in, we were proud to know he had done so well; he always worked very and hard never missed a day's work.

Christopher completed his year and gained his MA. We would have to travel to Leicester for his graduation and when the time came we were delighted to do so, Tamsyn joined us for this special occasion.

Christopher's plans were to move into the flat in Hornchurch which Tamsyn had already secured and he was to concentrate on filling job applications.

One day I had just come home from work, exhausted, as always, and was relaxing with a coffee when the phone rang. It was Stuart, who said 'Mum put the television on quickly there are the most dreadful scenes going on in America,' it was such a horrid scene to see unfold. I phoned Christopher and told him to put the news on; it was a day so painful for so many people it would be forever etched on our minds.

The next year was busy for Christopher and Tamsyn putting all their wedding plans together as all had to be booked so far in advance.

Some time later Ken and Linda, Tamsyn's Mum and Dad, invited us to spend a weekend with them so that they could show us the church and two choices of reception venue that they would choose from. Ken and Linda made us very welcome.

The next year Tony and I would celebrate our silver wedding – the same day as my friend Joan's 60th birthday.

Emma and Andrew, Joan's daughter and son, invited us to a celebration meal they had planned for their Mum.

It was very ironic that the sad news of the death of The Queen Mother should be at this time, as Joan and I had both worked at Clarence House, we realised that she had enjoyed a very long and mostly happy life, and the event brought back memories for both of us. As always it was lovely to spend time with Joan and Emma, my goddaughter, their family and friends.

Tony and I had planned to spend the actual day of our silver wedding with Betty and Brian in Swindon, though before that we had an anniversary surprise as Tony's Mum and Dad, Christopher and Tamsyn, Stuart and Kelly, Tony's sister and Clive and their four boys, had booked a special meal for us all in Broadstairs. It was so lovely and very special to be with them all.

We were also very spoiled by Betty and Brian with flowers and champagne and yet another meal. The sad part of the day was that it was the day of the funeral of The Queen Mother and I really did need to sit and watch that. I know Terry was very sad on that day, though no longer there at Clarence house; he was so loyal and devoted to her. So it was that I sat and watched the procession and felt a touch of sadness, and memories too, seeing some of the faces I knew who were still there from my days at Clarence House. Of course I also knew of some who were no longer with us.

The rest of the day we were able to relax and enjoy the company of Betty and Brian before going out for a nice meal that evening. Indeed it was a very memorable silver wedding anniversary.

The school meal ideas were changing and the company became more strict to assure things were done their way; I didn't like the intrusion as we had our kitchen running well with high meal numbers and a standard of food I liked, till now we had more or less done things our way and were left alone. This left me unsettled and having thoughts of leaving, one reason being I felt it would be easier to get a job before I was sixty as I was now in my late fifties. I told the girls of my thoughts and put in two applications, gaining one interview, it didn't feel right though, so I left it.

Mrs Waller was having another head teacher conference and again asked if I would do the buffet, of course on a non-school day. Once more it was very hectic and hard work, Tony was a great help as he wasn't working that day and Jan our caretaker did lots of washing up, again it was a great success enjoyed by all.

I was on the phone to my sister Bunty in Scotland who broke the news to me that our sister Mary had terminal cancer, I was devastated at the news and let Betty and Meg know. Over the next months it was heartache getting the news of the speed of her illness. Lesley often asked how the news was and if she was improving as I stood there making custard and fighting back the tears in my eyes as I told her Mary wasn't going to recover.

In December we got more sad news as Mary's husband Willie was taken into hospital, he had been frail for some time, in his eighties he was older than Mary who was in her late sixties. Bunty took Mary in to sit by Willie who said 'Mary it's been wonderful I wouldn't change a thing.' Later Willie passed away during the night; we felt he just didn't want to live without Mary.

As this was Christmas events time at the school I was sad to have to miss Willie's funeral; I think Meg did manage to go to Scotland and the rest of the family were there.

Christmas activities were hectic as always and I was horrified to wake up in the night before the big Christmas lunch actually being sick. There was no way I could let everyone down; I stayed sipping boiled cooled water and managed to stop the sickness. I got through the day feeling ill – sipping water all day and basically worked it off. I didn't have time to think of being unwell as we had three separate groups to cook for: normal lunch for the children, who enjoyed their Christmas lunch the day before Christmas lunch for the teachers and for the senior citizens had to be sent out.

This a marathon task at the best of times and more so when feeling ill. I felt both relieved and proud to have accomplished this to the high standard we always aimed for. These were my thoughts when it was over and as I walked to the church hall, where they liked me to call in as a thank you and receive a small Christmas gift, before going back to the kitchen where the girls were still busy clearing up. We really all worked so hard and it was late by the time we finished, I hate to think how many extra hours we put in unpaid for, though of course there was some extra time paid for these events.

It was nice to relax and unwind to enjoy our own Christmas, though this year had the sadness of losing Willie and of Mary being so very ill. Our niece Sandra was just so wonderful, she always had a great relationship with Mary and now looked after her so well, we would forever be in her debt.

We were in constant touch for news of Mary. Betty and Brian had a flight booked to visit; I too had plans for Tony and I to travel to Scotland in February half term. That was until the 1st of February 2003 as on Saturday morning I had a call from Betty to say Mary had lost her battle for life. I was truly heart broken, we had lost the dearest sister, most definitely one of life's good people; it was the very worst of days.

Arrangements were made for Mary's funeral to be on a Friday. I cleared it with my coordinator that the girls were happy to cook the lunches on the Friday and the Monday, with some changes to the menu, and Tony and I drove overnight on Thursday to Scotland, a twelve hour drive. We stayed with Chris and Eric, all the family and many friends were there. Everyone loved Mary and now there was a big hole in our lives.

On a lighter note, the next day we called into a supermarket and met Chris's daughter Marianne and her two children. Kyle, perhaps aged five, said to his Mum 'I saw my other Granny it was awesome!' Of course I wasn't his Granny but I did look a bit like Chris and it was a lovely light hearted moment.

After we got back I wrote a poem for Mary. I so often wrote poetry for any occasions, weddings, birthdays, etcetera. I now realise most of my family enjoy doing this, we all seem to have this love of verse – our Dad and Aunt too had this flair.

St Mary's was a Church of England school and our vicar was always in to take morning service. One day he came to me to ask if I would prepare a buffet for him as The Archbishop of Canterbury, Dr Rowan Williams, was to visit. I said I would be very honoured to do so, even if it was a day of school. I always did much of the preparation at home and I would have the girls to help with the rest. These events always took plenty of planning and lists, and Tony taking me to do the shopping.

This gave me an idea as the next year Christopher's wedding was planned and I wondered if I could ask the Archbishop to send a message of blessing for Christopher and Tamsyn on their special day. I took the chance and did just that, hoping it wouldn't be forgotten. I had written out all the details and was honestly able to mention Christopher's love of Canterbury Cathedral and all things history, including his continued involvement with The Dover Western heights Preservation Society and of Tamsyn's teaching post.

The buffet was fun to do, all the girls enjoyed doing the party food and it was a good success. The church ladies had to come and collect the food for the church hall.

Strangely, in all the times we'd done these special events I was fortunate that none of the management came in as I never cleared it with them as I should have done. They would have agreed but wanted it all done their way and I didn't want to be restricted to a few simple foods, that was not our way and everyone who requested a buffet always gave me the money to shop for the food with my own choices. Lesley, Lyn and Chris loved doing party food, as we were preparing them we were commenting on how we could have our own business in party food – a nice thought indeed.

We were still a very good team who worked well together and enjoyed our friendship, including all the great chats and hearing each other's family news, with plenty of laughs amidst all our hard work.

Stuart and Kelly called in to see us one evening, Kelly now lived with Stuart in his flat, and they had some news for us of their own.

They were going to have a baby! I have to say I was fairly stunned and a little concerned as Kelly was so young. I had tried to give them some advice when they moved in together, but who wants to listen to Mum!

It took a week to let it register for me before I told the girls at work, then one day I said 'you'll have to look after me now as I'm going to be a grandmother.' From then on it was an event to look forward to and we were all very happy. While sitting in a café with Tony's Mum and Dad I said 'how would you like to be great grandparents!' They were over the moon, as I knew they would be, and Sheila couldn't wait to start to knit – buying wool that very day. She made so many little jackets, all so lovely, and I started to knit some cot and pram blankets.

This meant the baby would be born the year of Christopher and Tamsyn's wedding, we now knew this was going to be a very busy year for us in many ways!

This was the year of Tony's Mum and Dad's Golden Wedding and we were going to have a family party at his sister Theresa and Clive's house. Theresa and I planned to prepare the buffet.

The first event of the year was going to be the birth of our grandchild, as on the night of the 8th of February Kelly went into labour. I was working the next day and feeling anxious for news, Stuart phoned me a few times, the girls too were eager to hear the news. Kelly had a hard time, she was really very brave as there were problems causing concern, the day felt very long – as I'm sure it was for Kelly and Stuart. It wasn't until 7.30pm on the 9th of February that Stuart phoned me to say their baby was delivered by caesarian section and they had a son, he was 9lb 3½ozs!

Tony and I went to the hospital to see Dylan Tyler who was stunningly beautiful, we were elated! Kelly must have been exhausted, I was full of admiration for her as she did have a very hard time.

Soon they were back home and Stuart was going to look for a bigger flat. They settled into some routine. I looked after Dylan lots while they were flat hunting. They came to live with us while they did up their new home and I looked after Dylan, he really was a very beautiful baby, something everyone who saw him commented on, he and I spent so much time together.

Our next celebration was the party for Tony's Mum and Dad in Theresa's house. It was a most enjoyable event, though I have to say my drinks were rather strong, with me blaming Clive, my brother in law. It was my own fault really and Nick has never let me forget that, as I was very chatty and 'educating' Nick on eating his five a day of fruit and vegetables! Even now he laughingly tells me he does eat his five a day. I lasted the night okay, it was really nice, and the only sadness was that Tony's Dad, Les, was becoming more handicapped by his illness. Tony and I spent much of our off duty times visiting to support them as much as we could and I spoke to Sheila every day on the phone. They were still able to come here when Tony picked them up and Sheila and I went downtown shopping, it gave her a break from being a carer.

The concern now was would Les be able to be at Christopher and Tamsyn's wedding. Sheila loved it when we took Dylan with us when we visited, she was so good with babies.

At half term this year I was going to Betty's as Swindon has a great shopping centre and Betty could help me choose my wedding outfit. As Tony wasn't off I travelled by coach and felt very grand to have such a smart hat box in my luggage on my return journey.

Chapter 24

Times of Change

As always, this was a busy year at work and I had much to think about with our family wedding.

I had known for a while that Lesley had thoughts of leaving as she found lifting the tables so hard on her back, but in fact Chris was first to leave us as she had been offered better paid work assisting disabled pupils at a grammar school.

We were very sad to have Chris leave, but would always see her in town. Our new lady was called Tracy and, after a time, she settled in and enjoyed her work. Then Lesley too was leaving some time later; like me Lyn didn't like to see our team break up. Again a replacement was soon found, this was Karen who came from South Africa. She was so lovely, she had two daughters at our school, and we were settled again though we knew that Karen may not stay too long. There always seemed to be changes these days and for some time Jamie Oliver was taking much interest in trying to make big changes in school dinners, things seemed to be more unsettled.

Other changes came about a few weeks later because of Joanne, our other EHO; which lead to big decisions. At the end of our days work, Fred, my coordinator, came in; it felt as if she was hovering waiting for me to go, it just didn't feel right. That day Tony was meeting me and we were going to his parents in Ramsgate. We hadn't driven far when I realised that I'd left my glasses and we went back. I hurried in to get them and there was both Fred and Joanne sitting with the meal registers. I was livid – why not just ask and say 'Alice we want to look at the books.' It felt as if they had sneaked in, I was very cross and insulted, I had nothing to hide and should have been there to answer any query. The rest of the day was spoiled for me as I was so upset; I was even sure that Irene had once told me that Fred or company staff should not ever look at the free meals register –

so this was all wrong. This was only three weeks before the end of the summer term. That night I had made a decision, I didn't even tell Tony, the next day I got most of lunch in order and then I phoned Fred and told her exactly what I thought of her behaviour. I then told her I was handing in my notice. When Lyn came in and heard this she was very upset, and when I told Mrs Waller she was furious and called Fred and Joanne in for a meeting. She too found them very disagreeable and she had never liked Fred. Joanne did say I don't want Alice to leave. Mrs Waller came in and asked if I would reconsider, I said 'no I've had enough of their insulting behaviour,' my mind was made up, so now I only had three weeks left at St Marys, I had been there thirteen years.

On Monday, Lyn said that she too was leaving, I tried to talk her out of it, but she wasn't going to work with another cook. Of course Tracy was upset, I said she must stay as she found the work was right for her and she would get used to a new cook. We also now had Peta but she was only temporary. I couldn't believe how fast and sudden it all seemed. I had really had enough and didn't like all the changes being talked of, as we had always been left alone and done things our own way.

At least I would be free to enjoy Christopher and Tamsyn's wedding.

All too soon it was my last day at St Marys, Mrs Waller told me I was to come in and attend morning assembly so I had to rush and prepare as much as possible for lunch.

I did feel very nervous when there was a chair for me on the stage with all the children and teachers in the hall. It was so lovely, two children from each class came forward to present me with their huge hand designed cards filled with drawings and messages. It was hard to hold my emotions in check. I received a lovely crystal bowl and shop vouchers and flowers, it was really very nice and I would enjoy reading all the messages when I was at home. When back in the kitchen I had so many flowers from children and parents, as well as messages and very touching letters from one or two parents. Later, nearing finish, Lesley and Chris came in, Mrs Waller said she was pleased as she felt we had been a great team. Lyn hadn't told anyone she was leaving and would put her notice in during the holiday.

Luckily Tony was coming to take me home as I had so many flowers it was like a florist, as well as the big cards and gifts. In the evening I felt emotional with so many lovely messages and lots of "we never needed Jamie Oliver in our school". The day had been full of emotion.

The next week I would buy a leaving gift for Lyn, and we agreed that we would meet up for a coffee now and then. It's always great to meet in with any of the team when in town.

Now the wedding was very near, I was delighted so many of my family from Scotland were going to be there as well as Meg, Paul, Betty, Brian and Gordon.

The wedding day was the hottest day ever, we felt sorry for the men in their morning suits.

Tamsyn's dream wedding dress was so lovely and she looked beautiful; the reception venue was perfect, the grounds so lovely and yes there was a letter from Lambeth Palace with a message and photograph of The Archbishop, which was lovely for Christopher and Tamsyn. They both really enjoyed their special day so much, as I'm sure so did all their guests. Bill, John and Eric looked great in their kilts. Tony's Mum and Dad were able to come; I was pleased especially as his illness was causing him so much distress and hard work for Sheila to look after him.

It was very hot having to stand for so many photos.

Especially for Christopher and Tamsyn, this was not the last celebration for this year as we still had Tony's 50th birthday and I was making secret plans for that. Dylan, who was seven months old, was good as gold at the wedding, he was such a joy to us.

It was strange not to think of going back to the school but I still needed to work. I got a job as cook in a residential home in Folkstone so had to take the bus home each day, Tony drove me there each morning, but oh dear did I miss my lovely kitchen at St Marys! Tudor Lodge was an old building and the kitchen was much in need of being modernised, I only stayed there three months as I saw a residential home in Dover needed a cook so I went for an interview, which was fine. I was taken to the dining room to fill in some forms when I heard some of the chat of the residents, one comment made me smile, on hearing one ask another how did you enjoy lunch he said, 'it was braised steak, tough as old boots,' oh dear, I thought this sounds fun!

After working my notice in Folkstone I started at Meadowdean, the kitchen again was not like St Marys but it was better than in Folkstone and I could walk if I needed or take a local bus.

I met lots of new people but did miss having my own team, it was hard to get used to and months before I felt I belonged, I made sure there was no tough meat! I was always in so much ahead of paid time, that wasn't a problem, gradually it became okay and I would do this until I retired.

Some of the carers were really nice girls and both managers were nice, now I was like Tony working every second weekend. There were two cooks: one on one off. I got to know Liz, the other cook, as I worked with her till my CRB check was cleared, but I didn't really like having a shared kitchen.

I had to work, that first Christmas and was able to show how I liked to prepare and display a buffet that was much enjoyed by all.

We got settled in our new routine, Tony and I. Sometimes I was off in weekdays, that was nice, and every second weekend we went to Ramsgate to Sheila and Les, so we were always very busy and I chatted on the phone to Sheila every day. It was getting harder for her being a carer for Les, it was so sad as Les was always such a good person and everyone liked him.

For Tony's fiftieth birthday I had booked a surprise meal. I chose a restaurant near to Tony's parents' house to assure that Les would manage to be there. It was an intimate and high quality place, there were sixteen of us, all our family, Theresa's family and Tony's godparents, Iris and Les, and of course ten month old Dylan. Tony was surprised and delighted, we had the happiest evening. Everyone had a lovely time and Dylan was, as ever, a delight, even the waitress fell in love with him.

There was one little mishap on the way home as Tamsyn tripped and fell, badly grazing her knee.

As I finalised the bill the owner said 'you have a wonderful family' – yes, I agree. Tony said thank you and how much he had enjoyed the evening.

In all it had been quite a year of celebration with the golden wedding, Dylan's birth, the wedding and Tony's 50th.

The next year Christopher and Tamsyn planned to start looking for a house so that they could move out of their hired flat.

Another year was almost at an end – how quickly the years pass, even more so on a busy year such as this.

With the next year underway, we had Dylan's first birthday on February the 9th. We were therefore sad to be told that Stuart and Kelly were going to separate, this was very upsetting, they were both still living in the flat for now but leading separate lives. Stuart had Dylan much of the time, I did worry and wonder about how it would all settle, I still looked after Dylan whenever needed. Kelly was going to find a home before she could have Dylan. Eventually they did get sorted; each parent shared time with Dylan, but I was sad for Stuart – especially when he needed to sell his flat. We were happy for him to move back home as long as he needed to, it wasn't the best time for him. We could see he was such a good Daddy and loved Dylan so much, spending all his free time with him.

There was another family wedding, Theresa's son Russell, and his bride was also called Kelly. Christopher, Tamsyn, Stuart and Dylan came to join us, Kelly looked so lovely and everyone had a great time.

With a lot of young children, Russell had hired a bouncy castle, Dylan loved that, and as it was near to their home Tony's Mum and Dad were able to be there to see their grandson marry, it was a wonderful wedding much enjoyed by everyone.

Working life was less busy than at the school, this being one of the reasons I left as I could work a couple of extra years in a lighter job, as my next birthday was my sixtieth.

At home we were having a new bathroom fitted, this created much upheaval especially when I had Dylan to look after, he was a toddler now and into everything, though he was always a delight, so gorgeous with blonde curly hair and perfect fair skin.

Towards the end of that year Tamsyn and Christopher had some nice news for us, they were going to have a baby. They were delighted as, I am sure, were her Mum and Dad who had their first grandchild to look forward to. Would Sheila get her wish for a great granddaughter? We'd have to wait and see, but once again she was busy with her knitting.

Les was much less well these days and it was very hard on Sheila, though he did spend a few hours at a day centre each week which gave her a break. Les had been such a young looking fit and healthy man with the very nicest of natures, it was hard to accept how things were for him now, it felt a cruel blow.

All that we could do was be as much support as we could, we had our work though we visited every time we were off, as did Theresa. It was a time of great concern.

The Western Heights Preservation Society, founded by Christopher and two friends, had grown from its humble beginnings from their first open day that attracted between forty and fifty visitors, making perhaps only fifty pounds. Tony and I made a decent contribution to this and it has grown so much and become a major attraction on open day for visitors to learn of the history of this major historic site. The key members still work very hard, now they have hundreds of visitors, while Christopher's work keeps him too far and too busy to continue, we're proud to know the start of it all and to hear of the society going from strength to strength.

In June of the next year we were eagerly awaiting news of the birth of our second grandchild. Christopher and Tamsyn had chosen not to know if the baby was a boy or girl, so it was very exciting to hear that their baby daughter was safely born and she was to be called Abigail Emma. So that was great news, we so looked forward to visiting and to see Abigail. Tamsyn was quickly out of hospital, we had to visit at her Mum and Dad's house where they were staying as some major repair work was being done on their own home, therefore it was unsafe for a new baby.

Sheila was so happy to have a great granddaughter.

We were getting very concerned for Les, who was much less able now. Tony and I did go there as much as possible as I am sure Theresa did too, it really was a difficult time.

I was pleased when Christopher and Tamsyn felt able to come to Dover and to visit Sheila and Les in Ramsgate, she was so happy to be able to cuddle Abigail, just as delighted when we brought two year old Dylan to visit. She loved babies and was very good with them.

On that visit Christopher and Tamsyn said they wanted Tony and I to visit on my birthday weekend, Tamsyn said treat yourself to a new dress as we'll go out for a meal, saying she would do the same! It was nice to look forward to.

Life for Stuart had settled to a new pattern after he and Kelly were no longer together. Stuart spent every off duty moment with Dylan, he was a perfect Daddy and Dylan seemed to accept the changes with no problem. He still spent lots of time with us and Stuart took him to his Nan and Granddad's lots if times.

I chose not to retire on my 60th birthday as I felt I could work another two years. This age did feel a real landmark. I knew we were having a celebration at Christopher and Tamsyn's so we would just enjoy a nice dinner at home on the actual day. We had Sheila and Les one of the days, now they only liked to come for a few hours.

It was fun getting ready to go to Essex; I looked forward to seeing how Abigail had grown. On our journey Tony said that we were a bit early so we would stop off for lunch, that alone surprised me as it was so out of character for Tony. I was in disbelief when at Maidstone he said we were half way now and turned off – I thought he would wait till we were at least in Essex to stop off. Then he drove into the car park of a really smart hotel, The Maidstone Hilton, I said 'aren't you overdoing it for a casual meal!' 'No' said Tony 'we are going to stay here tonight to celebrate your birthday.' It felt weird and I actually felt a pang of disappointment thinking that I wouldn't see Abigail! I never said this as I felt it would have sounded ungrateful, but to me it felt very strange and not like Tony. As he booked us in I was in a kind of daze, and he kept going out after he'd taken me to our room.

I still never guessed what was happening, we went to the lounge for drinks and a sandwich then I was stunned to see my lovely Dylan appear and say 'Grandma!' He and Stuart had come, then Ken and Linda, Tamsyn's parents, more friends and family, Alison and John, Theresa and Clive, Betty and Brian, Gordon too, a very big surprise was to see my brother Colin and his wife Jessie, of course Christopher, Tamsyn and Abigail. Twenty five friends and family came altogether, it was really lovely though I was still in shock. A meal had been booked for all of us and I never suspected a thing. Joan and Emma arrived in time for the meal. It was very special and very nice indeed, a most enjoyable event and to meet them all at breakfast next morning I felt very spoiled. Alison's son David came in later with his wife Jadie to bring me some flowers, very memorable and lovely, now I had lots of thank you letters to write.

I did work on for the next two years as planned, telling Sheila how we'd spend more time together when I retired. I talked to her every day and Tony and I went there every time we were off, she did need the support. Les tried so hard to chat with us, it was hard to see him so ill, they hadn't been able to be at my surprise meal, it would have been too much for Les.

We had Dylan with us every weekend, he was a delight – such a character, and so beautiful his lovely fair skin and blonde curls. He was, and is, a very precious person in our family and so at home here and he loved his Granddad so much. To see his little shiver of excitement one day as Stuart had him out on the path to await our arrival from work or another time when Betty and Brian were here and took us all out for a meal, she wanted Kelly to come too and it was really nice; Betty and I watched how Dylan's eyes followed his Granddad's every move as he went to the bar. Dylan was good as gold.

Stuart worked very hard and spent every spare moment with Dylan. During this time, he had met another young Mum with a little girl, Keira. It was some time before we knew of this and their relationship blossomed till they wanted to be together. Chloe was moving back to her home in Canvey Island and Stuart decided he was going to put in for a transfer from his work to the same firm in Basildon, and then he would move to Canvey Island. He was still going to come here every weekend from Friday to Sunday to be with Dylan.

It came to the time when it was clear that it was too much for Sheila to be able to care for Les at home. One night he seemed so ill that we feared we may lose him and Tony and Theresa spent the night at their flat to give their Mum a break, during that night they decided they would have to look into getting a good care home for their Dad. It hurt very much but it was the only way as both Theresa and Tony had to work. They went round some homes the next day and made some plans.

I said to Tony that I wanted him to mind his Dad one day and I would take Sheila out shopping as it was nearing Christmas and it did worry her that she couldn't get any presents bought, that plan was set and it would give her a break. Theresa said she would like to come too so the three of us had an enjoyable day, mostly it was for their Mum. We had a nice lunch out and she enjoyed the day. By this time we knew of two new babies that would be born the next year, both great grandchildren for Sheila and Les, as Theresa's daughter in law and Stuart's Chloe were both having babies, so that day Sheila bought gifts of a baby box for each of them and would do some knitting.

Some days later Les was taken into a home to be cared for, it was very hard for Sheila to accept, she went there every day and spent most of the days with Les. Now Tony and I had two visits to make and brought Sheila here to us for a Sunday now and then, it must have felt so strange being without Les. Tony's Mum had always been reasonably healthy, though very tired with being a carer.

This was not a very good time in our lives as we were concerned over Les and Sheila feeling so low, she and I still chatted on the phone at least once a day, sometimes more, always discussing family news.

It was just before Christmas when Sheila tripped on the step and hurt her wrist, the Doctor said it was sprained, but the swelling made us think different and it was actually fractured and so it was bound up. Now we were feeling concerned for her, she felt so low. I tried to cheer her up about how we'd go out when I retired the next year.

We all got through Christmas, that morning Tony and I went to his Mum taking breakfast with us and to let her open her presents before the three of us went to the nursing home to spend time with Les. Sheila was going on to have Christmas lunch with Theresa, and Tony and I were going home.

We planned to visit Christopher and Tamsyn in January and said we would bring Sheila, she would enjoy seeing Abigail.

Her wrist was still strapped up and she was feeling very down and not eating very well, we think she brightened up seeing Abigail, she was always so good with babies.

The next months were difficult as Sheila seemed so low – one day saying that she couldn't move. We raced there, the Doctor was called, Sheila's brother, also Les, and his wife Iris were there on our arrival, they would stay with Sheila while Tony and I visited Les and did some shopping for Sheila. I bought fish and vegetables and would cook it for her. The Doctor still hadn't been, she was a little better though didn't eat more than a mouthful. We had to leave, Iris and Les said they would be there when the Doctor came and would let us know. The Doctor assured Les and Iris that nothing serious was wrong. We would be there at the weekend and I talked to Sheila each day. A week later Sheila was no better, we were very concerned and the Doctor called her to her surgery for blood test results. Theresa's son Nick came to drive her there.

Some time later Nick phoned me to say his Nan was to go straight to hospital. I felt pleased to feel that she would be getting help to recover. Tony and I would visit the hospital that evening, I phoned Tony.

When there Sheila looked so poorly as she had tried to talk to us lifting her oxygen mask, that week was a round of work, hospital visits and going to visit Les. Theresa worked at the hospital, she was a ward sister, and was able to call in to her Mum, she phoned me each night to report how her Mum was. Things got worse and she was taken to the special care unit, the news wasn't very good. Both Christopher and Stuart phoned each night, concerned for their Nan.

Theresa phoned to say they were going to do a tracheotomy to help her breathe. We were very upset that this was not a success and at 4am Theresa phoned and said Tony should come to the hospital as their Mum wasn't going to make it. I was on duty that morning so chose to do breakfast and then get to the hospital; sadly it was too late my lovely Mum in law passed away at 8am. I was devastated, I had taken a taxi there but it was too late, Tony phoned me at 7am before I left for work he said it was only time, it was the very worst of days.

I got the news on arrival at the hospital, Tony and Theresa had already left to go and break the news to their Dad

We all spent the day with Les once Tony came to collect me. Iris and Les, her brother, came later in the day. We still had the news to break to Christopher and Stuart. The next weeks were busy with all the normal formalities.

Theresa and I prepared the food for after the funeral; the flowers were gorgeous, Sheila had always loved flowers.

I found it very hard to recover from our loss, I missed her so very much, in only six months I was going to retire and had thoughts that we would spend so much more time together and I missed our phone chats so much she was my closest confidante. It was hard too for Tony and Theresa as it was all so quick and unexpected.

Now of course we had the flat to empty and to sell to pay the fees for Les in his care home, as well as between us and Theresa we had to be there for Les and see to his needs visiting as much as possible.

This had been such a shock to us all it was hard to come to terms with.

I wrote a nice poem in her memory.

Over the next year we saw Les as much as possible, he still sometimes asked for Sheila, and whether she was going to visit as he sometimes forgot.

We loved having Stuart and Dylan most weekends and the two Mums to be would soon be adding to our family, it was sad that Sheila never did get to see the babies that she had bought baby boxes for and filled with useful items chosen on the day Theresa and I took her shopping.

Both babies were due on the same week. Theresa's first grandchild was first born, this was a little girl for Kelly and Russell, she was named Sophia; seven days later Chloe gave birth to Connor, a second son for Stuart, news for us all to cheer about.

We felt it was nice that Stuart and former partner Kelly managed to become reasonably good friends as this was good for Dylan to see that his Mum and Dad could be together when needed for his sake. Stuart had the closest relationship with Dylan and even with their strange circumstances he is the very best Daddy to both his boys, I have never seen a father who gives more time to his children. I am full of admiration and love for Stuart, they spend so much time being together and having fun, it has to be seen to be believed. Connor has had some serious setbacks through having asthma, he is still strong and looks healthy again so beautiful with his white blond hair and very fair skin.

We are so lucky to have three gorgeous grandchildren. Abigail has the most beautiful long hair that falls into ringlets. We are very proud of them all.

Debbie, our manager at work, wanted me to accept an offer to take a food course in nutrition. At this time I was nearing the time I had chosen to retire I hadn't wanted to mention it to her so early but worried to have them pay out for a course that may not benefit them, she did say 'I'd like you on the course' and so it was over the next three months I had plenty of paperwork to try to understand. As usual my confidence was low but once I got into the work I found it very interesting and indeed gained my certificate in ability to serve nutritional food. I was very pleased to feel that Alice, who left school with no special credits, had at least gained these with my basic and intermediate food hygiene and now this last one as well as the personal awards won while at the school – yes I liked that, it was a bit of a confidence boost.

Tony and I were going on a Rhine river cruise holiday with Betty, Brian, his sister Freda, and Doreen and Les – Freda's friends. We really looked forward to the break arranging with Theresa and Clive for extra visits to Les.

This was a lovely relaxing holiday we enjoyed in the very best of company going on some great outings, I loved going back to Titisee where Tony, our boys and I along with Chris, Della, Tony and Natalie had visited when our children were very young. I was sorry to see the changes in this wonderful setting, it was now spoiled being much more commercial, we still loved it and I sent Chris a postcard from there asking if she remembered this place.

One superb outing we loved was a tour of Salzburg by night on a special boat, it was magical.

Then back to reality, the rest of my time at work I was thinking of my retirement, now almost counting the months and having thoughts of how I would fill my time. I always knew I wanted to write my story telling of my life – it would be a great project for me.

I was going to buy a small desk for this; I also chose to commit to some voluntary work as a visitor for the partially sighted or blind. I loved chatting with people and hearing their stories.

My first lady was Joan, aged ninety, she was so special, the loveliest lady, we became real friends over the next three years. She was housebound and so loved my visits, sadly she passed away at the age of ninety two, she was a very proud and remarkable lady for her age – her mind so alert till the end of her life.

Chapter 25

Life Changes

My feelings were very strange and mixed in the days leading to my retirement, the loss of Sheila left an empty void, yet I looked forward to the freedom and was eager to start my writing. I had bought a desk, though felt I hadn't chosen wisely, Stuart was very amused at my complaint, the paper or book was impossible to keep on the slope front, he found that funny! I chose to just use the dining table and the desk for storage.

I had two more ladies who I visited weekly, it was a nice break from being at home, as I knew that I would miss the friends that I had made at work.

It was quite a while before I started on my writing, the hardest part being where to start. Eventually during the night it came to me and I couldn't wait to start. My best writing time has been to sit in the mornings, over the past two years it has been a great project, it has taken a world of patience and there have been plenty of mistakes but I have truly enjoyed it all.

A few times Tony's Dad was taken into hospital, we did have some days we could sit outside with him when visiting. We were upset to see he wasn't able to talk so clearly and that he was so forgetful. He did always ask how the boys were, we imagine he thought of them as the young boys he'd remembered not the grown men they now were. Les always had the most enviable thick curly hair, he was a great looking man, we were sad to have him like this.

We had a series of upsets in this year. The first was the shock of when my neighbour Margaret knocked to tell us that her husband Bob had passed away during the night, no illness, nothing, a big shock, we enjoyed a good friendship with our elderly neighbours. Bob and Margaret liked Tony and I so much and loved our well behaved boys who were teenage school boys when we moved in.

Then to know my brother Colin had suffered a heart attack while away from home, thankfully he had a successful operation and doing well, days later to get a call from Betty to say Geordie, our brother, had cancer he was going to have some treatment, again very distressing news.

I had seen Colin and Geordie the same day the year before when we went to Scotland for Colin's 70th birthday, we all had such a lovely night together with Colin and Jessie treating about forty of us to a lovely meal, Bunty was there too. I got a nice photo with Colin, Geordie, Bunty and I. Tony and I really enjoyed that night. Geordie seemed well then with no word of problems. It was a shame Betty missed that night as she had just returned from Scotland.

Over the next months we kept in touch to see how Geordie's treatment was going, he always phoned and spoke to Betty. When late November came he was having a serious operation and the signs were not very good, nothing more could be done to help, his condition was terminal. Betty said she wanted to visit so she and I decided to travel to Scotland on the overnight coach in early December, it was a very long journey. Betty's sister in law Freda kindly said I could stay with her too, it would make Betty and my visits to the hospital easier. We were heartbroken to see how ill Geordie was, though it was nice that he was able to chat with us. It was nicer the next day as he was moved to a much nicer ward in a nearby hospice and seeing our niece Pauline, Geordie's daughter, she was lovely and so devoted to her Dad. On our last day, before travelling back, Sandy's daughter Sandra came to visit. We hated saying goodbye and leaving Geordie knowing we wouldn't see him again, Betty and I were in pieces as we left, our other sisters and brothers all visited Geordie as well.

Freda's daughters were so good to us giving us lifts so much over those days.

The coach journey back was even more of a nightmare made longer by serious holdups through an accident in Aberdeen adding hours to our journey and both missing our connection bookings to Swindon and Dover.

In January we had plans to visit Swindon to help celebrate Betty's husband Brian's 70th birthday. Before this we were going to Billericay to spend Christmas Day with Christopher, Tamsyn and Abigail, only staying one night as Tony's Dad was taken into hospital ten days before. We were very concerned how we never saw him wake up during our visits, though we were upset when they talked of sending him back to the nursing home, to me that didn't feel right. We were lucky that Theresa was a nursing sister at the hospital, she said 'no that was not going to happen I'll sort it out' so he stayed in hospital with us all visiting as much as we could.

We got through Christmas and almost to the year end when the call came from Scotland that our lovely brother had passed away on the last night of the year, as this was a holiday period his family Pauline and Peter couldn't get arrangements made.

Tony and I did go to Swindon as planned, at least we'd be together to think of Geordie. We had a nice meal out to celebrate Brian's birthday.

Then it was back to Dover and Margate to see Tony's Dad. A couple of days later he had caught an infection and was moved to an isolation ward a day or so later. It was decided after consultation with us that, other than morphine, he would have no more medication.

Tony, Theresa and I sat with him for two days, us staying nights at Theresa and Clive's. The next day I came home for news of Geordie's funeral as with Betty and Brian I planned to fly to Scotland. During these days the weather became very severe causing many problems and flight cancellations. Tony needed to stay and be with his Dad. As it was, he lost his struggle for life on Friday the ninth of January during the night. Tony phoned me to say that he would be home the next day to take me to the coach station to London and Heathrow, we were lucky our flight was okay. Our brother's funeral was on the twelfth of January, the weather was very severe that year, the event was very upsetting, only nice to see all the family.

Tony kept in touch with news of his Dad's funeral, this was to be seven days later, for me two funerals in a week, not a good start to the year, both were much missed lovely people.

Later that year Tony and I were invited to spend a holiday in France with our friends, Rose and Mike, who had moved to the French Alps from Hawkinge, near to Dover. Rose was Tony's friend who worked with him before her retirement. We had spent enjoyable visits to their Hawkinge home before their move. In France we had a lovely holiday with them in their lovely mountainside home. Mike ran an owl sanctuary back home and had taken his owls with him to France. We had some lovely outings and Mike drove Tony and I to see the great views up in the mountains, it was a super visit, we loved it.

It was Rose that made bride and groom outfits for teddy bears for the top of Christopher and Tamsyn's wedding cake.

We do have another invitation to have a holiday in their lovely home and may do that one day.

Chapter 26

Tony

Special mention reserved for my husband of thirty five years. From the early days and our first meetings as he came in to see me at Clarence House.

He did find it very amusing to find me busy making Christmas crackers as he laughed at the items I had bought to put in them, they really were too big and were not helping my task. 'Oh well that's me when I have an idea!' I did always have some projects on the go, this he could have done so much better, at that time I didn't know of his artistic talent.

From the drawings that he did for Christopher and Stuart or making post-man's hats and bags with cardboard boxes and black tape to a realistic level, or the wonderful shop created from cardboard boxes enjoyed for months, this was a great talent. He is a great Dad to his boys. Of course in army life he was often away especially, when we lived in Germany.

Tony and I both share a calm nature creating a calm and peaceful environment for our boys to grow up in, I think this was very important as in turn over the years we have had many compliments on how well behaved our boys were and helped create the very nice young men they are today, we are very proud of both of them.

Tony's talents were much in use over my working years all those superb menus drawn for my work and even more so in our own home. In the early years in this house Tony completely renovated the garden and set himself the marathon task of digging out an area to create a sunken patio which Christopher and Stuart enjoyed helping him with. He then constructed a walled trough for flowers four foot in length to the height of our front garden having to make steps up to that our family cairn now being the central feature. It was all really hard work.

On the year of the Millennium I found a perfect gift for Tony, an especially smart album where I put photos of his school menus as well as those of him working on the garden restructure and of him sitting drawing the design for the glass we had made for our new front door as I wanted thistles along with our number – in other words a record of his talents. I say to him we can never leave this house because of our cairn and our front door!

At any time when we had a family birthday for our celebration we always chose to have a special dinner party to a very high standard with a beautifully set table (again by Tony). We do this for any special occasion these days mostly Tony and I for birthdays and anniversary days with good food nicely set table and soft music, that's just how we like it. These events make me think of my dear late friend Robert who I know would laugh at us and say 'do you think you are the Queen?' as he used to while we were at Clarence House as Helen and I or Greta, Pat and I loved to have special dinners. Robert loved a laugh.

Photos of Tony's table settings and his Christmas house decorations are also in the special album.

Christopher is like me in that he loves to cook and make special meals and try new recipes.

Tony and I planned to go on another holiday with Betty, Brian and Freda. Again we chose a river cruise this time on the Danube taking stops in Vienna, Bratislava, Budapest, Melk and Durnstein, another great and relaxing holiday and in great company.

Another highlight in Tony's life, this was actually before we met, was when as a young soldier in the mounted division he was chosen to go and be groom for Lord Mountbatten for two weeks. He had to live at his home, Broadlands, in Hampshire. This was a great experience for him. He did have some laughs, on arrival he was shown round the house and where to avoid setting the alarms off, then it was down to the stables, his workplace. Lord Mountbatten said to him 'there will be a film on in the cinema tonight, do join us.' Tony went there to find them all dressed in dinner suits and long dresses – there was him in combat trousers and his boots! He noted that though no one really bothered. It was late as he went to find his room he said the place felt so strange yet he was scared to switch on the lights as he couldn't remember the alarm switches and was terrified he'd touch the wrong one plus he couldn't be sure he knew the right way to his room, I could imagine this young teenage lad.

Another adventure while we were engaged. Once he was in Windsor Armoured Division they were going to Denmark on exercise and were given overseas allowance, fatal for a young troop of soldiers! They had a night out spending their money, boarded their ship on time, thankfully, then it was hit and a hole in the side meant the exercise was abandoned. They were brought home, money was to be given back; that's right, none of them had it, they had all spent it!

We were very upset in 1977, the year of our marriage, to learn of the bomb that took the life of Lord Mountbatten, Tony was pleased to be chosen to be on his funeral escort.

The many very funny stories over the years, often while away on exercise, that Tony was able to tell would almost be a book of its own so we always had plenty to talk of after his times being away. I think his tour of Canada was his longest spell away while we lived in Germany.

During that time Chris and I spent the time taking Tony, Natalie, Christopher and Stuart out for great fun walks or any of the trips that were specially booked for us, it was a lovely time before the children were tied to life as school children. I think a super time of freedom to bring them home from our walks or trips, nice and tired at almost bedtime and we could relax and unwind.

Now here we are; our children all grown up and my boys with children of their own. Chris has no grandchildren as yet, though Richard, her youngest, and our godson, is engaged.

Stuart is a very hard working young man who is never idle. He is devoted to his two sons, he spends most weekends here with us to be with Dylan, sometimes having Connor with him. It is nothing for them to spend seven hours out on outdoor activities – no doubt why my smart six foot son is a perfect weight as are his sons. I think of him specially today as it is his thirty second birthday. I feel proud of the way he and Kelly can, if need be, spend time together for Dylan's sake as it makes a difference to his life. In Dylan they have a bright young eight year old who is an absolute delight and has brought his Granddad and I much joy. Connor too, so lovely, although we see him less often, he and Dylan love to spend time together. Connor is four – a lovely, active little boy. They have a complex life but it works for them.

Christopher also works very hard, he is now curator of his museum since he was twenty nine though I rather liked his title before his promotion, Philatelic Curatorial Assistant, sounded rather grand (once I remembered it!). He travels into London for work and walks six miles each day. I can truly say they don't have a lazy bone in their bodies, both work so hard and also work hard at home too. He and Tamsyn love six year old Abigail so much, she is loving being at school and she loves books so much she may well be a great scholar.

On the Jubilee weekend Dylan and Abigail were both here. We put up an awning festively decorated and they had such a lovely time together that it was a joy to see, yes indeed we love our three grandchildren so very much.

My sisters and brothers all have grown up children too and enjoy being grandparents. I believe we have two weddings in Scotland next year, we still love to get together whenever possible as they are all so very important in my life, to have lost Mary and Geordie was very hard and they are always in my heart. It was a lovely and emotional touch on Christopher's wedding day a year after we'd lost Mary when Chris showed me a photo she had in her handbag and said 'Mary is with us Alice, I have her picture,' an emotional moment as she showed me.

Chapter 27

Reflections

It would be hard to believe how many words I have written and rewritten to reach this aim and I have loved all of it.

I can now reflect on some memories I haven't yet touched on, creating special moments in my life.

The many friends that I have met over the years, Robert will always be close to my heart. Terry, no longer with us, Mrs Syme, her son David keeping me informed in her last days, losing friends – that's the way life is I suppose. Joan, my first Clarence House friend, together with my goddaughter Emma, brother Andrew and Kim, we have shared many happy celebrations together, this makes me think back to the walks and climbs Joan and I enjoyed.

Alison and John, we shared so many joyous times together, in recent years John had a serious operation, I phoned Alison to ask for him saying 'I left it yesterday for your family' for Alison to say 'but you are family Alice,' how lovely and emotional was that, thank you Alison you will always be special.

As indeed are Chris, Tony, Natalie and Richard, I still love and care for you all.

Rose and Mike all important in my life.

Sandra, John and Sonja to laugh with them or cry with them, they all hold their special place in my life and I'm richer for their friendship.

Now I can think back to my days at Clarence House, The Balmoral Castle Dances, The Ghillies' Ball! I bet Carol hasn't forgotten the time her dress and The Queen's became tangled the footman had to untangle them.

I loved having attended all those special functions, to think when I see Royal Ascot, The Garter Service, garden parties, marching bands, The Trooping of the Colour or visiting dignitaries to feel I have an understanding of these events, an inside look I would not otherwise have had and from the army side too, all touches of life that has made it a little bit different.

Living in Germany, Tony, Christopher, Stuart and all enjoyed those years. I loved being a Mum and will love my boys in this life and beyond – I hope they will always feel that in their hearts.

Dylan, Abigail and Connor give Tony and I so much pleasure.

We love seeing them grow up and enjoy their childhood and look forward to seeing them aim for their goals in life.

Theresa, my sister in law, Clive, Russell, Nick, Craig and Calvin, we are so pleased to live near to them, they too are special to our lives and to see all their families grow.

I loved to meet in with any of the ladies who I worked with at the school, Jackie, Debbie, Carol, Lesley, Lyn and Chris to have a chat and talk of how our families are doing is always a pleasure.

Tony still has some years to work before his retirement now with a year added on through government plans. Our life is always full and busy.

I still visit two ladies each week, that keeps me busy.

When I get people that reply I still love to write letters though sadly so many people no longer do so now.

Mostly it is just Tony and I now for birthday and anniversary dinners, we still love to have those nice dinners with soft music playing to relax and create an atmosphere of love and well-being.

Most weekends we love to have Stuart and Dylan with us.

Every Sunday Betty and I chat on the phone and catch up with any family news.

I feel a great pride in all my family, none of my sisters or brothers were ever out of work, my brother John is now in his early sixties has been at his same job for all his working life.

With all the turmoil we endured throughout our childhood and because of the strength of our character in every one of us we have come out so much stronger.

I felt my life plagued by lack of confidence it grows and comes alive to know there is a certain kind of something special in the gallantry and sheer power in all of my family. I can't name it but can feel it and see it in all of us through how our lives are conducted in our ways, thoughts and behaviour and a knowledge that we have the right to be proud, feel pride and hold our heads up high. Looks and height were not our given gift but in our hearts there is a power and strength and a behaviour that creates a superior family with a real Rob Roy MacGregor spirit.